THE
COLOSSUS
OF RHODES

To find out more about the
Roman Mysteries, visit

www.romanmysteries.com

THE ROMAN MYSTERIES

by Caroline Lawrence

—— • —— A Roman Mystery —— • ——

THE COLOSSUS OF RHODES

Caroline Lawrence

Orion
Children's Books

First published in Great Britain in 2005
by Orion Children's Books
This edition published 2005 by Dolphin paperbacks
a division of the Orion Publishing Group Ltd
Orion House
5 Upper St Martin's Lane
London WC2H 9EA

5 7 9 10 8 6 4

The Orion Publishing Group's policy is to use papers that
are natural, renewable and recyclable products and
made from wood grown in sustainable forests. The logging
and manufacturing processes are expected to conform to
the environmental regulations of the country of origin.

A catalogue record for this book is available
from the British Library.

ISBN-13 978 1 84255 138 7

Typeset at The Spartan Press Ltd
Lymington, Hants

Printed in Great Britain by
Clays Ltd, St Ives plc

www.orionbooks.co.uk

To Faith and Al
for their *philoxenia*

— ITHACA —

When you set sail for Ithaca
Pray that the journey will be long
Full of adventure, full of discovery.
Don't be afraid of Scylla and Charybdis.
The Sirens and the Harpies
And even the Cyclops hold no danger for you.
You won't find such creatures on your journey
If your thoughts are high and you have a noble motive.
You won't find such monsters
Unless you erect altars to them in your heart.
Pray that the voyage will be a long one
With many a summer's evening when,
With such pleasure, such joy,
You enter harbours you have never seen before.
May you visit Phoenician markets and Egyptian ports
To buy pearls, coral, amber, ebony and gems of wisdom.
As you sip heady wines from the west
And inhale sensual perfumes from the east
Always keep Ithaca in mind.
Arriving there is what you are destined for.
Better if the journey lasts for years
So that you are old by the time you drop anchor there,
Wealthy with all you have learned on the way.
Ithaca will not make you rich.
She gave you your marvellous journey.
She has nothing more to give you.
Without her you would never have set out.
So if you find her poor, it's not because she fooled you.
You will be so rich with experience
That you will finally understand
What Ithaca really means.

written by Constantine Cavafy (1863–1933)
paraphrased by Caroline Lawrence

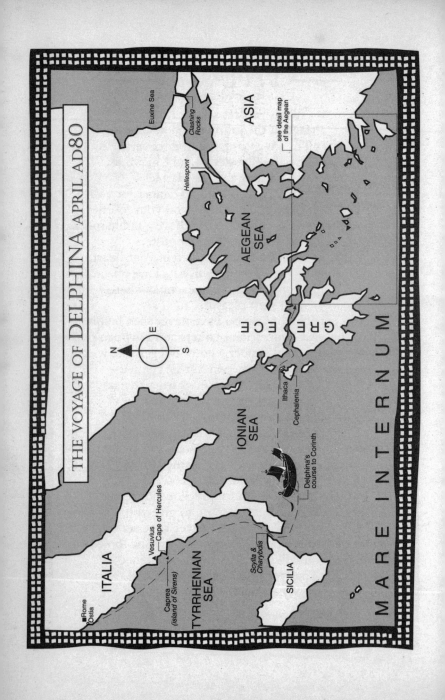

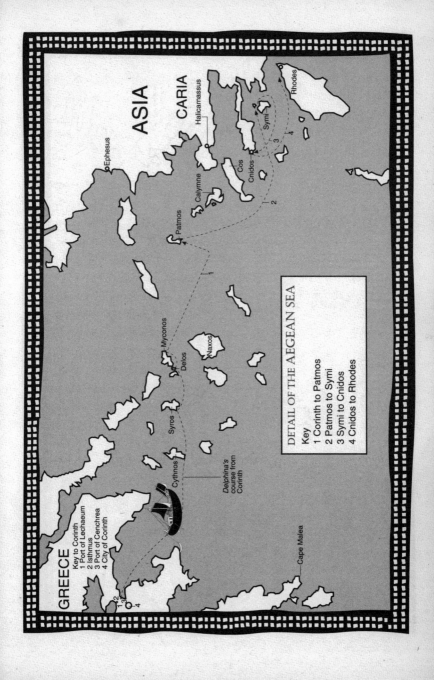

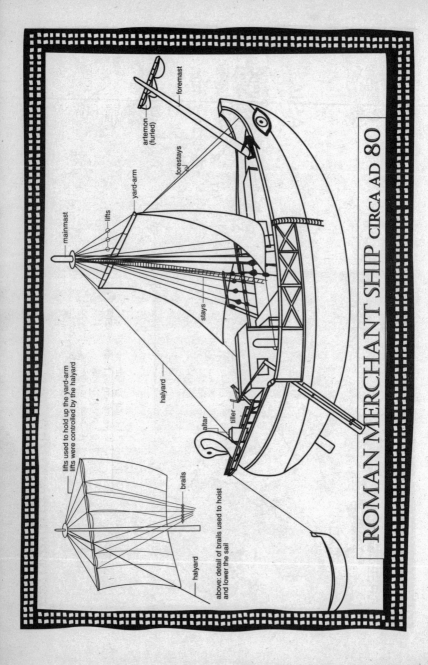

ROMAN MERCHANT SHIP CIRCA AD 80

foremast

artemon (furled)

forestays

yard-arm

lifts

mainmast

stays

halyard

altar

tiller

lifts used to hold up the yard-arm
lifts were controlled by the halyard

brails

halyard

above: detail of brails used to hoist
and lower the sail

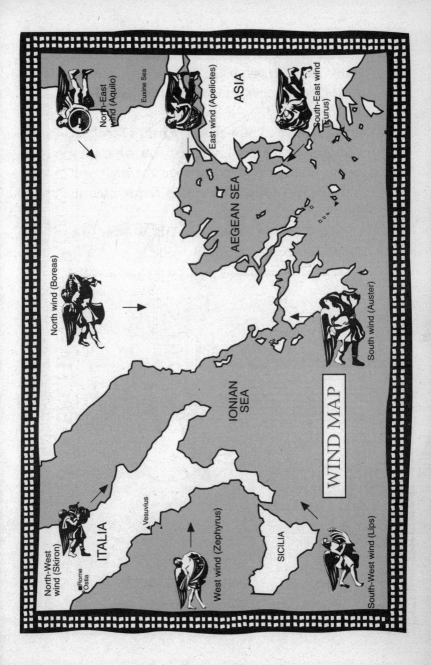

This story takes place in ancient Roman times, so a few of the words may look strange.

If you don't know them, 'Aristo's Scroll' at the back of the book will tell you what they mean and how to pronounce them. It will also explain some of the ship terms used in this book.

Maps at the front will show you the *Delphina*'s route.

SCROLL I

Lupus stared in amazement at the little bronze pendant hanging from its linen cord.

It was shaped like a part of the body.

Part of a boy's body.

A very *private* part of a boy's body.

Lupus glanced up at his three friends standing beside him in the early morning sunshine on Ostia's marina pier. Each of them had just been handed a similar pendant.

Flavia Gemina, the highborn daughter of a Roman sea captain, had already put hers on. Her former slave-girl Nubia – dark-skinned and golden-eyed – was hiding her pendant in cupped hands and giggling. And Jonathan ben Mordecai stared at his with mouth wide open in mock astonishment. When Lupus saw the expression on Jonathan's face, he barked with laughter.

'Stop it, you three!' hissed Flavia, touching her light-brown hair to make sure it hadn't come unpinned. 'You'll hurt Alma's feelings. You know very well these aren't rude. And they're not funny, either. They're powerful good-luck charms.'

Flavia's house-slave Alma folded her plump arms and nodded. 'That's right. They're amulets to ward off the evil eye.'

'Thank you, Alma,' said Flavia. 'It was very thoughtful of you to get these for us.' She shot the others a significant look.

'Er . . . yes. Thank you, Alma.' Jonathan slipped the amulet over his head so that it hung beside the herb pouch which gave him relief from asthma. He grinned. 'I'm sure these will be very protective.'

'Thank you, Alma.' Nubia was still giggling. 'Mine has little wings on it,' she said to the others.

Alma nodded and beamed. 'Wings make them extra lucky. So do bells.'

Lupus grinned and gave his pendant a shake, so that it tinkled. His amulet was obviously the best because it had wings *and* bells.

'They're apotropaic,' said the children's tutor, slinging his leather satchel over one shoulder. Aristo was a good-looking young Greek with sad eyes and curly hair the colour of bronze.

'What is apple tropic?' asked Nubia. She had been in Italia for less than a year and her Latin was not yet fluent.

He smiled at her. '*Apotropaic* is a Greek word,' he said. 'It means something that turns bad luck away from you.'

Alma nodded. 'That's right. They're tapo . . . pota . . . they're what he said. Seeing as what you four have been through recently – mad dogs, volcanoes, pirates, assassins, plague, fire, wild beasts and I don't know what else – well, I thought it was time you had something to protect you.' Alma spat and made the sign against evil. 'After all, a sea voyage is far more dangerous than any of those other things!'

'Oh, Jonathan! It will be dangerous? You need go?'

Lupus and the others turned. Jonathan's mother Susannah was picking her way through the bags and satchels on the wooden pier. When she reached Jonathan she pulled the blue veil away from her lovely face, and Lupus saw that her eyes were red and swollen.

'Mother!' hissed Jonathan. 'I just said goodbye to you and father at home. I *told* you that you didn't need to come to the docks.'

'Your father says bring medicine, in case of emergency or sick.' Jonathan's mother handed him a linen shoulder bag. Then she pulled a handkerchief from the long sleeve of her light-blue tunic. She murmured something in Hebrew, spat gently on the handkerchief and rubbed it on his chin.

'Ow!' Jonathan jerked his head back. 'It's not a smudge!' he said in Latin. 'It's a scar from a sword cut. And it still hurts like Hades!'

'Jonathan, do not curse and please do not shout at me.' Susannah's beautiful eyes filled with tears.

'I'm sorry, mother.' Jonathan sighed. 'But I'm not a baby. I'm eleven.'

'But I love you so much, my dear, dear son.' She took his face between her hands and began to cover it with kisses.

As Lupus watched them, he remembered how distant Susannah had been with him the month before, when everyone thought Jonathan was dead. He also remembered the vow he had made.

'I think I lose you forever,' Susannah was saying to Jonathan. 'Then I find you but now you go away again.' She began to weep. 'Why you go away? Why you leave me now?'

'Don't cry, mother,' said Jonathan, glancing at the

others. Lupus knew he was embarrassed by his mother's clumsy Latin. 'We'll be back in a few months. Flavia's father says maybe even by the end of May.' Jonathan rolled his eyes at Lupus. But he submitted to his mother's embrace and said something to her in Hebrew as he patted her back.

Lupus felt a strange tightness around his heart. He had not seen his own mother for three years, since he had been kidnapped by the man who murdered his father. Venalicius the slave-dealer had cut out Lupus's tongue to stop him from talking and kept him prisoner aboard the slave-ship *Vespa*. But Lupus had finally managed to escape, here in Rome's port, far from his home on the Greek island of Symi. Dazed by pain and grief, he had lived for some years among the tombs on the outskirts of the city. During those years of begging and scavenging Lupus quickly learned to understand Latin.

Then, last summer, three children had befriended him. Flavia Gemina, a brilliant ten-year-old who liked to solve mysteries, her African slave-girl Nubia and their Jewish next-door-neighbour Jonathan. After their first adventure, Lupus moved in with Jonathan and joined the others for daily lessons with Aristo. Within months he had learned to read and write Latin, and also Greek – his native language.

Now that it was April, and the sailing season had begun, Lupus was about to fulfil his uncle's dying wish. He and his friends hoped to find and rescue the free-born children that Venalicius had kidnapped and illegally sold as slaves.

Beside him, Flavia and Nubia had knelt on the warm wooden pier to hug their dogs. The members of the

Delphina's crew were saying their goodbyes, too. A dark haired youth of about sixteen was kissing his parents, and a plump old woman was pinching the cheek of a scrawny sailor in an embroidered felt cap.

Lupus turned away. There was nobody for him. Nobody to care if he lived or died on the voyage. Nobody to offer daily prayers for his safety. Nobody to look out over the water and wonder where he was. At this moment he would even have welcomed Alma's squishy embrace, but she was hugging Flavia and weeping loudly.

Lupus's throat tightened, and to his dismay he felt tears prick his eyes. He went quickly up the gangplank of the ship and stepped down with his right foot first. Keeping his back to the others, he crossed the deck and gripped the polished oak rail.

As he gazed out over the water, he remembered the secret altar he had made on the beach three days before. He remembered the feel of the damp sand as he formed it into a cube as high and wide as his forearm. And how easy it had been to twist off the pigeon's head and tip out its blood, like dark wine from a twitching feathered jug. The waves would have washed away his altar by now, but he hoped that the blood he had poured onto it would fix it permanently in the memory of the gods.

Now, fingering his new good-luck charm, his tongue-less mouth soundlessly formed the words of the pledge he had made over the blood-splattered altar.

I will find you, mother, Lupus silently vowed, *and we'll be together again. And I will never, ever come back to this place!*

SCROLL II

'Where's your father?' said Aristo to Flavia as he came back down the gangplank onto the dock.

Flavia pulled away from Alma's arms and turned to look at her young tutor. 'I'm not sure. He was going to make a dawn sacrifice at the temple of Castor and Pollux, and then see the harbourmaster. But that was over two hours ago. He should be here by now.'

Aristo jerked his head towards the ship. 'Our paying passenger has just arrived and he wants to know when we set sail.'

Flavia shaded her eyes against the early morning sunshine and looked around the busy marina. 'There's pater!' she said. 'Just coming out from behind the customs stall, near those men pulling the mule.'

Marcus Flavius Geminus was a tall, fair-haired Roman of the equestrian class. Although it was not fashionable for men of his social standing to choose the career of captain, Flavia knew her father was happiest at sea. But he did not look happy now.

'Is everything all right, pater?' she asked, following him up the gangplank. 'You look worried.'

'I'm fine,' he said, stepping carefully onto the deck. 'Remember: right foot first,' he added.

6

Nubia and Jonathan followed Flavia onto the ship and Lupus came over to join them.

'Was the sacrifice all right?' Flavia asked her father. 'It wasn't blemished, was it?'

'No, my little owl.' He gave her a distracted smile and began to unwrap himself from his toga. 'The sacrifice was fine, but I still feel . . . uneasy. I don't suppose . . . did any of you dream about owls or bears last night?'

Flavia glanced at her friends. All four of them still had nightmares about the terrible things they had seen at the games in Rome the previous month.

But Jonathan shook his head and Nubia said, 'My dreams are fuzzy. I think I was being chased by Venalicius the slave-dealer.'

Lupus took out his wax tablet, his main method of communication, and he wrote: I DREAMT I WAS SWIMMING WITH DOLPHINS

'Dolphins are good luck,' said Flavia's father, folding his toga, 'but slave-dealers are bad. And today's Thursday. It's never good luck to set sail on a Thursday. Also, it's an even day of the month. Maybe we should set sail tomorrow.'

'But, pater!' hissed Flavia. 'We performed the *lustratio* yesterday morning and had the feast last night and we've said our goodbyes and now we're all ready to go.'

'And the wind is perfect,' added Aristo, gesturing towards the north, where a plume of smoke drifted gently away from Ostia's lighthouse.

Lupus pulled his lucky pendant from under the neck of his sea-green tunic and gave its tiny bronze bells an emphatic tinkle.

'I'm not sure.' Flavia's father ran his hand through his light-brown hair. 'I can't risk offending the gods.'

Flavia sighed. Since her father had lost his ship and crew the previous summer, he had become obsessed with signs and portents.

'Captain Geminus! Wait!' A short man of about her father's age was hurrying up the gangplank. He had thinning hair and pale brown eyes.

'It's Marcus Artorius Bato, the junior magistrate,' murmured Flavia. 'What's he doing here?'

'He's not a junior magistrate any more,' said Jonathan in her ear. 'His term finished at the end of December.'

'Right foot first!' cried Flavia's father, as Alma, Susannah and the dogs followed Bato down onto the deck. 'Step onto the deck with your right foot first, everyone, or you'll bring bad luck!'

'Captain Geminus,' said Bato, dropping his heavy leather satchel on the deck. 'Is it true that you're about to set sail for Corinth and Delos?'

'That's right,' said Flavia's father.

'Do you have any room for passengers? I can pay.' Bato touched the small leather pouch at his belt.

'Of course. But I'm not sure when we'll set sail.'

Bato took Captain Geminus by the arm and drew him aside. 'Listen. I had a visit from a friend of mine and his wife yesterday. Their two little girls have gone missing. And another girl disappeared a few days ago, an innkeeper's daughter, though I've only just found out about it.'

'Our baker's son is missing, too,' said Alma, who had pushed close enough to hear.

'Porcius?' gasped Flavia.

Alma nodded. 'He's been gone for three days. His father thinks he went to Rome to see the games so he isn't worried, just angry.' She looked at Bato. 'But what if Porcius hasn't run off to Rome? What if he's been kidnapped?'

'Kidnapped?' cried Susannah, clutching Jonathan's arm. 'Someone kidnaps children?'

'Shhh!' hissed Bato, glancing around. 'Please keep your voices down.'

Nubia's amber eyes were wide. 'Venalicius!' she whispered. 'He is back like in my nightmares.'

'Don't worry, Nubia,' Flavia slipped an arm around her friend's shoulder. 'It can't be Venalicius. He's dead. But maybe there's a new slave-dealer in town.'

Bato nodded grimly. 'My friend and his wife suspect kidnapping,' he said. 'I've just been to see the harbour-master. According to him, a Greek ship set sail without authorisation yesterday at noon.' He glanced round at them with his pale brown eyes and then added, 'A fisherman claims he heard children on board, crying.'

'Oh, the poor things!' Jonathan's mother started weeping again.

'Great Neptune's beard!' muttered Captain Geminus.

'Pater, we have to go today!' cried Flavia. 'While the trail is still fresh!'

'She's right,' said Bato. 'That ship might lead us to the mastermind behind these illegal operations. I thought I cracked this ring last year. But I was obviously wrong.' Bato shook his head and muttered. 'He must have agents everywhere.'

Flavia could still see the doubt in her father's eyes and she had a sudden flash of inspiration. 'Don't forget, pater, we promised Lupus's uncle. And we don't want to break a promise to a dying man. It might anger the gods and bring *bad luck*.'

Lupus's brass stylus made sticky noises as he urgently pushed it through the beeswax coating of his wooden writing tablet.

'Perhaps you're right,' said Flavia's father. 'Perhaps this is a sign from the gods.'

Lupus showed his wax tablet to Captain Geminus, and Flavia craned her neck to see it.

IT'S MY SHIP, Lupus had written, AND I SAY WE SAIL TODAY!

SCROLL III

As the *Delphina* moved away from the pier, Flavia and her friends waved goodbye to Ostia.

They stood at the back of the ship, on the stern platform beside a small altar to Venus and a large swan ornament. Usually the wooden bird's head gazed down at a little skiff trailing behind – like a mother swan with her cygnet – but at the moment the *Cygnet* was still towing its mother out of the harbour. The *Delphina*'s four-man crew were rowing while Flavia's father stood behind the deckhouse and steered.

But Flavia was not watching her father or the crew.

Her eyes were fixed on Scuto, an alert golden form sitting on the dock between Jonathan's mother and Alma. Nipur was a black shape running back and forth, straining at the lead in Alma's hand. But Scuto's patient face – Flavia could still see the tiny dots of his dark eyes – was even more heartbreaking than Nipur's frantic barks.

Flavia glanced at Nubia. Her friend's cheeks were wet and there was such a look of yearning in her amber eyes that Flavia could barely hold back her own tears. She stifled a sob.

'It's not too late for you to change your minds and go back,' said Flavia's father over his shoulder. He stood a few feet behind them at the helm, holding a rod of polished wood attached to the steering paddles. By moving this tiller he could guide the direction of the ship. 'I'd be much happier knowing you were safe at home.'

'No, pater,' sniffed Flavia, her eyes fixed on Scuto. 'We're saying goodbye of our own free will. The kidnapped children didn't have a choice. They didn't even get a chance to say goodbye to their dogs or their families. We have to find them.'

From behind her came a low voice. 'Why do *you* have to find them?'

Flavia turned to see Bato.

'Because freeborn children shouldn't be kidnapped,' she said. 'It's not right.'

'Of course it's not right. But you should leave it to the experts.'

'And being an ex-magistrate makes you an expert?' said Jonathan.

Bato raised his pale eyebrows. 'I'm surprised to see you on board, Jonathan ben Mordecai. I thought your mother only recently returned home from abroad. Don't you want to spend time with her?'

'I . . . we . . . she and my father haven't been together for ten years. They want to get to know each other again.' Jonathan flushed. 'I thought it might be easier for them if I wasn't around.' He took a breath. 'Also, I want to help find the kidnapped children.'

'I, too,' said Nubia.

'We all do,' said Flavia. 'It's our quest!'

Lupus folded his arms and grunted his assent.

Bato sighed. 'No, I didn't think I could talk you out of it,' he said. 'But listen to me. This particular investigation could be extremely dangerous. Don't tell anyone what you're up to. And for Jupiter's sake don't let anybody on board know the real reason I'm here. The official story is that I'm taking a holiday after my year as junior magistrate. Understood?'

They all nodded.

'Good. If you happen to get any information, tell me. But discreetly. Remember, I'm just a passenger. Just an ordinary tourist. Who's that?' He nodded towards a young man rising up from the hatch into the brilliant sunshine.

'Him?' said Flavia. 'He's just a passenger. Just an ordinary tourist.'

Bato narrowed his eyes at her, then gave a half-smile. 'What's his name?'

'I don't know.' Flavia shrugged. 'Pater told me but I've forgotten it.'

'Never mind,' said Bato. 'We'll soon find out. He's coming this way.'

Flavia studied the young man as he came towards them across the moving deck. She remembered seeing him and his slave-boy come on board, but she had been too busy saying goodbye to Scuto and Alma to take much notice.

He was tall and muscular, with dark eyes and floppy dark hair. The two broad stripes on his short-sleeved tunic told Flavia he was a patrician, like Bato. She guessed he was a little younger than her tutor Aristo, about eighteen or nineteen years old. He was very good-looking, so she gave him her prettiest smile.

The young man ignored her smile and went straight up to Bato.

'Hello,' he said in a deep cultured voice. 'My name is Gaius Valerius Flaccus.'

'Marcus Artorius Bato,' said the other. 'Let me introduce you to Flavia Gemina, the captain's daughter, and her friends Jonathan, Nubia and—'

'How long do you think it will take us to reach Corinth?' said the passenger, not even looking at Flavia. He was chewing some kind of gum or resin.

'Four or five days,' said Aristo, stepping up to join them on the crowded platform. 'That's if the wind is favourable. It will take a week to ten days if not.'

Flaccus nodded and moved to the rail. As he did so, he jostled Flavia. She fought back an urge to thump him hard.

'Big oaf,' she muttered under her breath, and gave him a withering look.

But Flaccus was oblivious. He had rested his forearms on the polished stern rail and chomped his gum. 'My father left me a nice legacy,' he remarked, 'and I thought I'd see the Seven Sights before I begin to practise law in Rome.'

'Oh, I know the Seven Sights!' cried Flavia, her desire to show off overcoming her irritation. 'They're the famous monuments which everybody says you must see before you die. Some people call them the Seven Wonders of the world.'

'From Delos I plan to go on to Rhodes or Alexandria,' said Flaccus to Bato and Aristo, with barely a glance at Flavia, who had begun to count on her fingers.

'There's the statue of Zeus at Olympia,' she began. 'the Mausoleum at Halicarnassus, the Colossus of—'

'Let's go down to the main deck,' said Flaccus abruptly to Aristo and Bato. 'We can talk more easily there.'

'How rude!' hissed Flavia when the three men had left the stern platform.

Lupus nodded.

'I didn't tell him there would be four children on board,' said Captain Geminus. He glanced over his shoulder at them. 'Flaccus is very rich and he's paying me well, so keep out of his way.'

'Happily,' muttered Flavia and then made her voice deep and cultured: '*My father left me a nice legacy,*' she said, mimicking Flaccus and pretending to chomp. '*I thought I'd see the Seven Sights before I become a pompous lawyer up in Rome . . .*'

Lupus laughed and Jonathan grinned.

Flavia snorted. 'Look at him, chewing like a cow. And Flaccus is a stupid name. It means big-eared or flabby.'

'Well, he doesn't have big ears and he certainly isn't flabby,' said Jonathan. 'He's got more muscles than most gladiators I know.'

'Then it must refer to his floppy hair.' Flavia clenched her fists to make her biceps big and flipped an imaginary fringe out of her eyes: 'I'm Gaius Vapidius Floppy,' she breathed huskily. 'But you can just call me Floppy.'

'Flavia . . .' Her father's warning tone.

But it was gratifying to hear her friends laugh. Laughter made her feel better, too. It took her mind off the memory of Scuto sitting patiently on the dock, already longing for her return.

★

When Nubia could no longer see Nipur she dried her tears, took a deep breath, and turned to face forward.

It was strange being on this ship again, the same vessel that had taken her far from her family and desert home. Without its hated yellow and black striped sail, the ex-slave-ship *Vespa* looked more like a cheerful beetle than a wasp. Now re-named the *Delphina*, it had a round hull and two masts, one of which stood straight up in the middle while the other leant forward from the prow. Both masts now carried white sails, not yet loosened to catch the wind.

Although the ship belonged to Lupus, Captain Geminus had been working on her for months. He and his men had sanded the peeling brown hull and brightened it with a fresh coat of blue paint. They had scrubbed the deck to a silken finish and waxed the oak rail until it was smooth as glass. They had polished the *Delphina*'s brass fixtures so that they shone like gold. And they had set up a small altar to Venus next to the swan's neck ornament here at the back of the ship.

Nubia realised she had been holding her breath. Now she let it out with a long sigh.

'Are you all right, Nubia?' Flavia's arm came around her shoulder and Nubia smiled and nodded.

'Yes. I think I will be all right.'

At that very moment a rising breeze ruffled the tawny fur on her lionskin cloak. Captain Geminus must have felt it, too, for he shouted out an order.

Within moments the crew was back on board. Nubia and her friends moved aside as a big sailor holding a rope ran up onto the platform. He bent over the stern rail to tie the skiff's tow-line to a heavy brass ring. Now the *Cygnet* bobbed below them in the *Delphina*'s wake.

The sailor straightened up and grinned down at them. Nubia had heard the other men call him Punicus. Although he was as hairless as a baby and as bald as an egg, his sleeveless blue tunic revealed powerfully muscled arms and shoulders.

'My special knot,' he said in his curiously light voice, 'so the little *Cygnet* won't drift away.'

He jumped back down onto the main deck as Flavia's father issued another series of commands. Nubia and the others turned to watch.

All four crew members had run to the hemp ropes which would release the sails.

Upon Captain Geminus's order, Punicus and a greyhaired Greek sailor named Atticus loosened the small white sail at the front of the ship. Then it was the turn of the two sailors at the mainmast.

'Who's the young one?' breathed Flavia. 'The one with the wavy black hair? He's as handsome as Paris.'

'He may be pretty,' said Jonathan, 'but he isn't as good as the one with the striped cap: *his* side of the sail is coming down much more quickly.'

'The man with the cap is Zosimus,' said Flavia's father. 'He's a Rhodian. And the boy is Silvanus.'

Flavia and Nubia glanced at each other and giggled.

'Silvanus is from Ostia,' continued Flavia's father, 'He's never sailed before. I couldn't afford to be choosy,' he added under his breath. 'This ship is thought to be illomened.'

The mainsail was unfurling now and as the wind filled it, Nubia clapped her hands in delight. 'Look! There is a dolphin on the sail. Were you painting it, Lupus?'

Lupus nodded.

'It's wonderful!' said Flavia. 'When did you do it?'

'We did it a few days ago,' said Jonathan. 'The day you two went shopping with Alma. We laid out the sail on the dock and I had to stop people walking on it while Lupus sketched the dolphin with charcoal. Then I helped him fill in the outline with black paint.'

'It is most charming,' said Nubia.

Lupus looked pleased and Flavia said, 'With the wind ruffling the sail like that, the dolphin really looks as if he's leaping through the water.'

Nubia pointed. 'And look at the bubbles coming up from his head.'

'That's where Tigris ran across the wet paint,' said Jonathan with a grin. 'Those bubbles are his paw-prints.'

'Jonathan,' said Nubia. 'Where is the Tigris? Why did he not come to say goodbye to you with your mother?'

Jonathan turned away from her and leaned his fore-arms on the polished rail, as Flaccus had done a few moments earlier. 'I thought it might worry Tigris if he saw me sailing off,' he said. 'Remember how upset he was the last time I disappeared?'

'Yes,' said Nubia. She was about to add that Tigris had almost died of longing but instead she pressed her lips together.

A moment later, she heard Aristo call them to lessons. Nubia turned with a secret smile and followed her friends down onto the main deck. At least there was one good thing about being on board the ex-slave-ship.

BEGINNING WITH YOU, BRIGHT APOLLO, I WILL DESCRIBE THE ADVENTURES OF THE HEROES OF OLD, WHO SPED IN THE SWIFT ARGO AFTER

THE GOLDEN FLEECE, PASSING BETWEEN THE CLASHING DOG-ROCKS

Lupus looked up from his wax tablet as Flavia laughed.

'No, Lupus,' said Aristo gently. 'Not dog-rocks. Blue rocks.'

The four friends and their tutor were sitting at a polished pine table fixed to the deck between the hatch-cover and the foremast.

'I can see how you made the mistake,' said Aristo to Lupus. 'You thought you saw the Greek word for "dog-like" – *kyneios* – rather than *kyaneas*, which means "dark blue". But you ignored two *alphas* and you supplied an *iota* where none existed. You have to look at every letter when you're doing a translation.'

'Letters in a translation are like clues in a mystery.' Flavia nodded wisely. 'Even the smallest ones – like *iota* – are important.'

Lupus glowered at her. He was Greek, and knew perfectly well what *iota* was.

On the table, the papyrus scroll rattled under the strengthening breeze, so Aristo placed a hand on either side of the open portion. 'This poem is called the *Argonautica*,' he said. 'It was written over three hundred years ago by a man called Apollonius Rhodius. Although Apollonius originally came from Alexandria in Egypt, we call him the Rhodian because he settled on the island of Rhodes. He may even have got an idea for one of his monsters there. The bronze giant Talos might have been inspired by the Colossus of Rhodes.'

Flavia nodded. 'I know about the monsters Jason had to overcome on his quest,' she said. 'There were the Sirens, and the Harpies, and Scylla and Charybdis.

Though really Charybdis is a whirlpool, not a monster. And then there were the rocks that clashed together every time a ship sailed through but the argonauts managed to escape by sending a dove through first so the rocks clashed together but as they began to move apart again Jason told his men to row as fast as they could and they just made it but the rocks crunched some of the wood on their stern!'

'That is what clashing dog-rocks do?' whispered Nubia.

Aristo laughed. 'I've told you, Nubia, there's no such thing as dog-rocks.'

But even as he spoke, Nubia heard a sound that made the back of her neck prickle. It sounded like the faint echoing bark of a dog.

SCROLL IV

Jonathan's stomach sank as he heard the muffled sound of a dog barking.

'Hark!' cried Nubia. 'Did you hear that?'

'Yes!' cried Flavia, her grey eyes wide. 'It was an eerie sound.'

Lupus nodded, frowned and tipped his head to one side.

'I didn't hear anything,' said Jonathan quickly, and then, as the faint barking came again. 'I didn't hear that either.'

'It sounds like there's a dog down in the hold,' said Aristo.

'Great Neptune's beard!' roared Captain Geminus from his post at the helm. Jonathan glanced back and saw him hand the tiller to Punicus and stomp towards the box-like covering of the hatch.

'Wait!' Jonathan slid off his bench and lunged for the hatch-cover. 'Captain Geminus, I can explain—'

But someone was lifting the cover from underneath.

Jonathan groaned. He wasn't surprised to see his dog Tigris, whom he had commanded to 'Stay in the hold behind these bags and don't make a sound!' But he was surprised to see the person who held Tigris's lead.

It was a boy of about fourteen with dark slanting eyes

and straight blond hair long enough to brush his lightly tanned shoulders.

'Look what I found!' laughed the boy, showing white teeth. 'He was tied up in a dark, damp corner.'

'Zetes!' called a deep voice from the stern platform. 'Leave that dog and come here at once!'

'Coming, master!' The boy dropped Tigris's lead and ran lightly across the deck towards Flaccus.

'What was my first condition of agreeing to take you with me?' boomed Flavia's father in his sea captain voice. She had rarely seen him so angry.

'No dogs,' said Jonathan, staring miserably at the deck.

'So why did you disobey me?'

Jonathan said nothing. Lupus held up his wax tablet: I DON'T MIND DOGS ON MY SHIP

'That is beside the point! We had an agreement.' Flavia's father took a deep breath and closed his eyes. Presently he opened them again and said in a lower voice: 'Dogs eat as much food as people. They require exercise. They need to have their mess cleaned up. And they have fleas.'

'I'm very, very sorry, sir.'

'I'm tempted to put him ashore at Three Taverns.'

'Oh please don't do that, pater!' cried Flavia. 'Tigris is a good watchdog and ratcatcher.'

Her father sighed and ran a hand through his light-brown hair.

'Jonathan.'

'Yes, sir?'

'You'll swab the deck every morning and evening. Clean up any mess that dog makes and share your own food with him. You'll also keep him quiet and out from underfoot. Is that understood?'

Jonathan nodded, his head still down. 'I will, sir. Thank you.'

'And now,' said Captain Geminus, 'please get back to your lessons.'

'Who is that boy?' asked Nubia, as they sat down again on the polished bench. 'He is most beautiful.'

'He must be Floppy's slave,' said Flavia. 'What did he call him?'

'Zetes,' said Nubia.

'Isn't there a Zetes in the story of Jason?' said Flavia.

Aristo nodded. 'He was one of the argonauts. Zetes and his brother could fly.'

'Hey!' cried Flavia. 'That gives me an idea. Let's play a game!'

Lupus reached for his dice-cup at the end of the table and rattled it hopefully.

'Not that kind of a game, Lupus. Let's pretend we're on the *Argo*, searching for the Golden Fleece and that everybody on board is a member of Jason's crew.' She opened her wax tablet. 'It can be part of our lesson. Can we do that, Aristo?'

'Actually,' he said, 'that's not a bad idea. Linking characters in a story with real people is a useful mnemonic.'

Nubia opened her mouth but before she could ask the question Aristo said, 'A mnemonic means a way of remembering. Go ahead,' said Aristo, folding his arms across his chest. 'Who's who?'

'Well,' said Flavia. 'Zetes is obviously Zetes.'

'Obviously,' said Jonathan.

23

'And I think pater should be Jason,' added Flavia.

Lupus shook his head vigorously and pointed at himself.

'But you're too young to be Jason,' said Flavia.

Lupus shook his head again and got up from the bench. He planted his feet wide on the bright moving deck and gestured round the ship and then pointed back at himself.

'It *is* his ship,' whispered Jonathan. 'I think he should be Jason.'

'Good point,' laughed Flavia. 'After all, Jason owned the *Argo* and you—'

'Shhh!' said Jonathan. 'Nobody's supposed to know Lupus owns this ship.'

'That's right,' said Aristo. 'Your father said it might undermine his authority if the crew found out he was taking orders from an eight-year-old boy.'

Lupus held up nine fingers.

'Sorry,' said Aristo. 'A nine-year-old.'

'You can sit down now, Lupus!' Flavia tugged the fluttering hem of his sea-green tunic. 'We agreed you can be Jason.' She wrote on her tablet and presently – after a lively discussion – Flavia held up the list, neatly etched in the yellow beeswax on facing leaves of her tablet.

ON BOARD *Delphina*	ON BOARD *Argo*
Lupus *the ship-owner is like*	**Jason,** *the Brave Hero on a Quest*
Flavia *Gemina is like*	**Atalanta,** *the speedy Heroine*
Jonathan *would like to be*	**Peleus,** *a Hero and father of Achilles*

Nubia has agreed to be	**Hercules**, because both wear lionskins
Captain Geminus (a twin) is	**Castor**, Pollux's mortal Brother
Aristo (a talented musician) is	**Orpheus**, whose Lyre tamed Beasts
Bato (former junior magistrate) is	**Mopsus**, a Wise Soothsayer
Flaccus (aristocratic snob) is	**Acastus**, arrogant son of King Pelias
Zetes (Flaccus's slave-boy) is	**Zetes**, the Hero who could fly
Silvanus (the handsome youth) is	**Hylas**, young Squire of Hercules

(Zetes is also very beautiful and some people thought he should be Hylas but he is already Zetes and besides, Silvanus is handsomer)

Atticus (old and Greek) can be	**Argus**, who built the Argo
Punicus (Phoenician helmsman)	**Tiphys**, Helmsman on the Argo

'I think that's everybody,' murmured Flavia, studying the list with satisfaction.

'What about that little man with the striped cap?' said Jonathan, pointing up towards the rigging.

ZOSIMUS IS FROM RHODES wrote Lupus on his own tablet.

'He has pigeons,' said Nubia.

'Pigeons?' said Flavia.

Nubia nodded. 'I see him bring them onto the board. Look!' She pointed towards the front of the ship.

'There are pigeons in that cloth-covered crate by the anchor?' said Flavia.

Nubia nodded. 'Zosimus tells me I can help him look after them. I ask him before we sail away.'

'Perfect!' cried Flavia. 'On the *Argo*, one of the

25

sailors released a bird which flew through the clashing rocks.'

'Do you remember his name?' asked Aristo.

After a moment of silence Lupus snapped his fingers. EUPHEMUS he wrote.

'Well done, Lupus!' Aristo patted Lupus on the back.

'You fee muss?' said Nubia, reading over Lupus's shoulder.

'Close enough,' laughed Flavia, and made an addition to the list:

Zosimus *(keeper of pigeons)* is	**Euphemus**, *a bird-loving Argonaut*

Jonathan frowned. 'I wonder. If we're not sailing through clashing blue dog-rocks, why did Zosimus bring pigeons?'

Nubia lay in the *Delphina*'s hold, wide awake.

Her stomach was pleasantly full of the beef and raisin stew they had eaten for dinner. The hammock was comfortable and the ship's gentle rocking had already lulled her friends to sleep. Tigris lay below them on some of the bags of Ostian salt they had brought with them; she could hear him snoring. Nearby, a swinging lamp-horn filled the hold with a soft apricot glow.

But Nubia could not sleep.

Up on deck she had been fine. Captain Geminus and his men had transformed the slave-ship so that the *Delphina* bore no outward resemblance to the hated vessel that had taken Nubia from her native land.

But they had not done anything to change the inside, except load the ship's hold with amphoras of fish-sauce, crates of glassware and bags of salt.

The moment Nubia had descended into the ship's dark belly the memories had come slithering back.

It was here in this very hold that the slave-dealers had stripped her, shaved her head and clamped a cold metal collar around her neck.

It was here they had beaten her.

And it was here they had strung a heavy chain through a ring on her collar and through the collars of other girls and women, so that a dozen of them were linked to each other. Nubia would never forget the constant jangling sound of those chains, their cold weight or their cruel tugging. Those at either end had been chained to posts or beams so that none of them could move more than a foot either way. They had no hammocks and there were only two positions they could adopt: sitting with their naked backs against the rough timbers or lying on the damp wood.

Once the chains were on, they did not come off. Nubia and the other captive women had not even been allowed to relieve themselves. Instead they had been forced to lie in their own filth.

Of all the humiliations, that had been the worst.

Every morning one of the slave-dealers would appear in a painful glare of light to sluice them down with buckets of gaspingly cold seawater. They were allowed a cup of drinking water only twice a day, and leathery bread only once. They ate so little that soon they did not need to relieve themselves. But then the hunger had begun, twisting like a dagger in their bellies and forcing pathetic whimpers from their throats. One night an old grandmother from the Gazelle Clan had moaned all night for 'a morsel of bread please, just a little morsel'. The slave-dealers had not understood her words. Even if they had, they would not have given her bread.

The old woman's silence the next morning had been more terrible than her cries the night before. But it wasn't until three days later that the men unchained her body and threw it overboard.

Nubia remembered something else. There had been a beam above her head with a pattern of knot-holes and flaws in the wood. From a certain angle it resembled a woman's face wearing a sad but kind expression. Once Nubia had 'seen' this face she could not unsee it. So she pretended the face was her mother's. And late at night, while the other captives slept, Nubia would speak to it and weep.

Now, swinging gently between her friends, with their steady breathing on either side, Nubia looked for the face-pattern on the wooden beams.

Suddenly she saw it, right above Lupus's hammock. Only a foot or two away. She was lying in almost exactly the same place as when the slave-ship first took her far from her family and her native land.

'Oh my mother,' she whispered in her own language, as the hot tears rolled from the corners of her eyes down into her ears. 'Please help me not to be afraid. Outside this ship is *Delphina*, but inside it is still *Vespa*.'

BEFORE LONG THEY SAW ANTHEMOESSA, HOME OF THE SWEET-VOICED SIRENS. HALF-WOMAN, HALF-BIRD, THESE SIRENS PERCHED HIGH ABOVE THE HARBOUR AND TEMPTED TRAVELLERS TO STAY FOREVER.

'An excellent translation, Lupus,' said Aristo. 'Next line, Flavia?'

But Flavia had risen from the bench and was standing on tiptoe to see over the port rail. It was an hour past dawn and they had just passed the Bay of Naples, with Vesuvius still smoking under its angry cloud. Now a jewel-like villa on the Cape of Hercules was coming into sight. Flavia's heart was beating fast, for the Villa Limona was the home of the first man she had ever fallen in love with. Was he there? She could clearly see the painted columns and domes and the tops of palm trees. But there was no smoke from the bath house – nor any other sign of life – and she wondered if he had gone to Rome for the games.

'Flavia?'

'What? Oh, sorry.' She lowered herself back onto the bench and gazed down at the scroll. 'Um . . . it says that Orpheus played music to drown out the siren's deadly song. But why are we reading this part?' she said, looking at the number on the end of the scroll. 'We've jumped ahead to book four.'

Aristo smiled. 'Today we're studying this passage of the *Argonautica* because we're about to pass the Island of the Sirens.' He pointed with his chin. 'There it is. Caprea.'

Aristo laughed as they all left the table and ran forward to gaze over the starboard rail. The breeze whipped their hair and tunics.

'Look, pater!' cried Flavia, pointing. 'The Island of the Sirens!'

'Better be careful,' joked scrawny Zosimus from the rigging. 'I think I see some lovely ladies on the rocks there. And they're not wearing much.'

Flavia laughed, then clapped her hands in delight. 'Let's play music like Orpheus did. To drown out the seductive song of the sirens.'

Lupus nodded and Jonathan raised both eyebrows. But Nubia began to cry softly.

'Nubia!' said Flavia, 'What's the matter?'

'I am tired,' she whispered. 'All night long I can not sleep.'

'Poor Nubia!' Flavia put her arm around her friend. 'Don't you like sleeping in a hammock? I love it. I slept like a rock. Or a fluffy cloud!'

'I do not sleep like a fluffy rock,' said Nubia quietly. 'The boat does not like me.'

Lupus's head jerked around and Jonathan said, 'What do you mean?'

'Yes,' said Aristo, joining them at the rail. 'What do you mean by that?'

'There is something bad on this boat,' said Nubia, pulling her lionskin cloak closer round her shoulders. 'Something evil.'

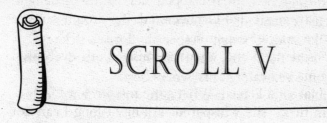

SCROLL V

Later that afternoon the sky grew cloudy and a shower came weeping down from the north, sending them down into the hold. The squall passed, but the temperature had dropped and the wind had veered. Now the *Delphina* began to pitch and roll, and when they went back up the wooden stairs Jonathan had to grip the rail with one hand and help Tigris with the other.

Up on the breezy deck, Jonathan saw Punicus at the tiller and Captain Geminus coming down the rope ladder. 'We're about to pass between "Scylla and Charybdis",' said the captain, jumping onto the deck. 'Look! There's Sicily.'

The dark bulk of land seemed to rise and fall beyond the starboard rail as the ship yawed. Jonathan took a deep breath and made his way across the swinging deck to join Aristo and the two passengers.

Flaccus and his slave-boy were sniffing wedges of an expensive yellow fruit called lemon.

'You look slightly green, Jonathan,' said Aristo. 'Are you feeling nauseous?'

'Hey!' cried Flavia brightly. 'The word "nauseous" actually comes from the word *naus*, which means "boat" in Greek. So nauseous literally means boat-sick.'

'Are you boat-sick, Jonathan?' asked Nubia.

He shrugged.

Flaccus extended his lemon wedge. 'Smell this lemon,' he said. 'I bought it specially for sea-sickness.'

'No,' said Bato. 'It's better to have a good vomit. Drink some seawater. That works best.'

Jonathan shook his head. There was nothing in his stomach to throw up. Since his return from Rome the month before, he had been training himself to stop eating at meals before he was satisfied, like a wolf whose hunger makes him constantly alert. But he had felt slightly sick ever since they boarded the *Delphina* and hadn't eaten anything in nearly two days. Jonathan patted his stomach. Beneath his tunic it felt flat and rock hard. He had the usual headache, dry lips and tender skin that accompanied a fast, but even so he felt good. Good because he had vowed never to be chubby again and he did not have a spare ounce of fat on him.

Leaving Tigris with the others at the rail, Jonathan found an empty patch of deck to do his exercises. He had learned them at the gladiator school and performed them twice a day to stay in shape.

He lay face down on the moving deck, put his hands beneath his shoulders and pushed himself up. His left shoulder still ached from an old brand and a recent wound, but he ignored the pain. He inhaled as he lowered his forehead until it was just above the deck, then exhaled as he pushed back up. He could now do almost one hundred of these before the muscles of his arms and shoulders burned with cold fire.

Jonathan ignored the jokes of the sailors as he did his squats. He had learned to shut out the world and focus on his body. Stretching his arms out before him and lightly touching the rail he sat on an imaginary bench, then stood, then sat, then stood. It was hard to do this on the swaying deck but he knew it was good for his balance as well as his muscles.

Finally, he tried the new task he had set himself. He had seen Zosimus go up one of the thick ropes called 'stays' as nimbly as a monkey. One end of the stay was knotted around a heavy bronze pin fixed to the rail, the other attached to the top of the mast. Now Jonathan approached the slanting rope, wrapped his legs around it and started to pull himself up. It was harder than it looked and he had only pulled himself a yard or two before his left arm started to tremble. The breeze was stiff up here. He paused for a moment, then forced himself to go higher.

Suddenly he stopped as a terrible smell filled his mouth and nose. It was the hot stench of rotten eggs. His heart was beating hard, now, but not with the exertion of the climb. It was pounding with fear.

Jonathan knew that sulphur smelled like rotten eggs. He also knew that for those like him who suffered from asthma, the smell of sulphur could mean death.

Lupus sniffed the air like a dog, then looked at the girls in alarm. The last time he had smelled sulphur a volcano had erupted. They all heard the cry and the thump, but Lupus was the first to reach Jonathan.

His friend lay on the deck, eyes fixed and chest rising and falling as he breathed in great tearing gasps.

'Dear gods! What's wrong with him?' said Flaccus.

'Is it his asthma?' said Captain Geminus.

Lupus nodded at them, and as Nubia knelt behind Jonathan and lifted his head onto her knees, he quickly found the herb pouch and held it close to his friend's nose.

'I'll get his medicine,' cried Flavia, and ran towards the hold.

Jonathan's chest rose and fell and his face was white, tinged blue around the mouth.

'By Hercules,' said Bato, 'He's like a fish out of water.'

Lupus kept the herb pouch close to Jonathan's nose and gently pushed a whining Tigris away. He knew his friend needed every ounce of concentration to suck air into his lungs. Jonathan had once told him that when the attacks came it was as if his lungs were wet sponges. And that huge gulps of air brought only tiny sips of relief.

At last Flavia was kneeling on the other side of Jonathan, bringing a copper beaker to his mouth and helping him take little sips. The tincture of ephedron was ten times as powerful as the herb pouch and presently Jonathan's breath began to come more easily. Finally, he relaxed onto Nubia's lap and closed his eyes. He was still wheezing, but Lupus knew he would be all right.

Suddenly, Zosimus uttered a strangled cry from the rigging above them. 'It's an omen!' he cried, 'A bad omen!'

Lupus looked up at his pointing arm, then ran to the rail.

The late afternoon sun threw shafts of orange light through breaks in the clouds so that the bubbling water was an unnatural bronze. But it was not the strange colour of the sea that had alarmed the sailors. Hundreds of fish had risen to the surface and were floating on their sides in the turbulent water.

'Charybdis!' Flavia cried, rising to her feet. 'It's the whirlpool Charybdis! It's going to suck us under!'

'By all the gods,' Lupus heard Bato utter an oath and saw him make the sign against evil.

'The fish look as if they've been boiled alive,' said Aristo.

'What's happening?' Jonathan wheezed, and Nubia helped him sit up.

'I've seen this before,' called Captain Geminus. 'It's not a whirlpool. Just bubbling water. Keep calm, everybody! Punicus! Hold your course. We should be fine once we're through the straits.'

Lupus leaned over the *Delphina*'s rail. He was fascinated by the variety of creatures floating in the sea. As well as the corpses of fish, he could see eels and a turtle and something else. Something enormous. It might have been a small whale or a huge shark. Whatever it was, it was almost as long as the *Delphina* and it was so close it nudged the ship's hull. Lupus leaned further over the rail, to try to get a better look.

'Lupus, you fool!' bellowed Captain Geminus. 'Get down from there!'

Lupus was used to the *Delphina*'s swinging motion by now, but he did not expect the violent forward jerk. He only managed to keep his balance for a heartbeat.

Then he felt his stomach lurch as he lost his grip on the polished rail and plunged towards the boiling sea.

SCROLL VI

'Boy overboard!' squealed Punicus from the helm. 'Boy overboard!'

Flavia got to the rail just in time to see Lupus's startled face speeding out of sight behind them.

'Pater!' she screamed. 'Do something!'

But her father was in complete control.

'Hang on everyone!' He ran to the helm. 'I'm going to bring her about! Atticus! Prepare to drop anchor!' Captain Geminus took the tiller from Punicus and pushed it hard to the right. The *Delphina* groaned and tilted sickeningly as she swung round into the wind. The stifling smell of warm sulphur filled Flavia's throat and made her retch. She gripped the rail with white-knuckled hands. A moment later the *Delphina* shuddered as the wind spilled from her sail.

'Drop the anchor, Atticus!' she heard her father's strong voice. 'Zosimus! Silvanus! Take in the sail!' And then, 'Punicus, take the helm. I'm going down to the skiff.'

Flavia watched her father slide down the rope which attached the small rowing boat to the *Delphina*. When he was in the skiff he quickly untied the rope that attached it to the ship and soon he was rowing away from them with long, deep strokes, striking dead fish with every sweep of his oars.

'Look!' cried Nubia. 'There he is! I see the head of Lupus.'

Despite her father's powerful strokes, the skiff seemed to crawl across the seething, fish-choked water.

'Oh hurry, pater!' cried Flavia. 'Hurry!'

'Lupus . . . is a good . . . swimmer,' gasped Jonathan, now on his feet and gripping the rail.

'But who knows how hot the water is,' said Flaccus, absently sniffing his piece of lemon. 'It seems to have cooked those fish.'

Flavia shot him a furious look.

'Perhaps the water is only warm,' said Aristo. 'It might be the sulphur fumes making it bubble.'

'Yes,' said Bato, 'and that might be what killed the fish.'

'He's there . . .' Jonathan wheezed. 'Your father's reached him!'

'Oh, please let him still be alive,' whispered Flavia, as she watched her father pull the small form into the skiff.

'I think I see him move!' whispered Nubia.

'I'm sorry!' came Silvanus's breathless voice behind them. 'The rope slipped out of my hand and it made the ship peck like . . . like a chicken! And I saw him fall . . . Oh dear gods!' He buried his beautiful face in his hands.

'Wasn't your fault,' said Zosimus, taking off his felt cap and making the sign against evil. 'It's this ship. She's ill-omened. This voyage is doomed.'

'Shhh!' hissed Flavia angrily. 'Don't say that!' But she couldn't ignore the feeling of dread as the little boat carrying her father and Lupus slowly approached the *Delphina*. Presently Flavia felt the skiff bump up against the side.

Zosimus cast down the rope ladder and climbed over

the rail. A moment later he passed Lupus up to the strong brown arms of Punicus, who lowered the dripping boy carefully onto the deck.

'He's alive! Oh, Lupus, you're alive!'

'And you are not cooked!' said Nubia.

'Back . . .' wheezed Jonathan, 'Give him . . . air.'

Flavia saw Flaccus turn and frown at Jonathan. 'I think you're the one who needs air.' Flaccus dropped his lemon and reached out just in time to catch Jonathan as he collapsed again.

Three days later, Flavia sat cross-legged on the stern platform in the shelter of the swan's smooth neck and gazed down at her friends. The three of them were in the skiff with Atticus and the beautiful slave-boy Zetes, fishing for sardines. Tigris lay panting beside Flavia, and the rattle of dice and click of counters from the deck told her that the three men were gaming at the table.

Flavia had wanted to be alone to collect her thoughts. She was making a list of all the accidents which had occurred in the three days since they had encountered the sulphur water. She offered up a silent prayer of thanks to Castor and Pollux for saving Lupus from the water and Jonathan from the fumes. Then she frowned down at her wax tablet. Apart from ropes that constantly seemed determined to trip them and odd lurching movements of the ship that often threw them to the deck, there had been a fire in the galley and two separate incidents of the water barrel breaking free of its rope. Two nights ago, Punicus – who knew the night sky like the back of his hand – had fallen asleep at the helm. Was Zosimus right? Was the voyage ill-omened?

Had they set out too soon without waiting for divine approval?

Flavia shook her head. They had carefully performed the *lustratio*, purifying the *Delphina* with the ashes of a bull, a fabulously expensive sacrifice. Her father made his offerings morning and night at the little shrine beside the swan's neck.

Was the ship itself evil, as Nubia thought?

Then a new idea occurred to her. Maybe it wasn't the ship itself that was malevolent, but something on board. She had heard stories of how *lemures*, the spirits of the dead, sometimes haunted a place where they had been unhappy. The *Delphina* had carried many slaves. And some must have died on board.

Flavia shivered and made the sign against evil. Almost three days ago they had left the safety of the coast. For two days and nights they had seen no land, just the vast plate of blue around them and the immensely high bowl above. They had been alone in the world and although the wind filled the *Delphina*'s sails and the water hissed constantly along her bow, there had been little sensation of progress.

Flavia knew this was the most dangerous part of the voyage, when there were no landmarks to be seen. Luckily, the night skies had been clear and the constellations had pointed the way. For the hundredth time she wondered: would they ever see land again?

This time, her question was answered by a cry from above.

'Land ahead!'

She looked up to see Zosimus pointing towards the horizon before them.

Her father left his place at the tiller and ran up the

rope ladder as nimbly as a boy. 'Praise the Twins! It's Greece, all right!' he called down to them. 'The island of Cephalenia.' He laughed. 'We'll be passing Ithaca soon.'

Flavia knew his last remark had been for her benefit. Ithaca. The island of the Greek hero Odysseus.

She slipped her wax tablet into her belt pouch and left Tigris keeping watch on the stern platform. As she emerged from behind the mainsail she saw that Bato, Aristo and Flaccus had left their game and beaten her to the prow. She hesitated. She liked Bato and Aristo, but she couldn't bear Flaccus. He was spoilt and arrogant and he had ignored her from the first moment he came on board. But unless she wanted to climb the rope ladder, the prow was the only place to catch her first glimpse of Greece. Quietly she stepped up onto a coil of rope directly behind Flaccus, so that he wouldn't see her from the corner of his eye. She was so close to him she could see the sheen of oil he had rubbed on his smooth tanned neck and she could even smell its musky cinnamon fragrance.

Aristo was pointing and Flavia looked over Flaccus's muscular shoulder to see a smudge on the horizon.

That must be it.

Greece. The land of myths and heroes. The land of gleaming cities, sacred groves and breathtaking wonders. Soon she would set foot on Greek soil for the first time in her life. She was pleased to find her heart beating fast.

'*When you set sail for Ithaca, pray that the journey will be long, full of adventure, full of discovery.*' Flaccus was reciting a poem in his deep, soft voice. '*Pray that the voyage will be a long one, with many a summer's evening when, with such pleasure, such joy, you enter harbours you have never seen before. May you visit Phoenician markets and Egyptian ports to buy pearls, coral, amber, ebony and gems of wisdom. As you sip heady wines from the west and inhale sensual perfumes from the east, always keep Ithaca in mind. Arriving there is what you are destined for.'*

Flavia shivered with the beauty of the verses, and Bato voiced her thoughts.

'That's superb,' he said.

'Whose is it?' asked Aristo, 'I've never heard it before. Is it Horace? Or Ovid?'

'It's mine,' said Flaccus, and added, 'One day I hope to win the ivy crown.'

Flavia could hardly believe what she was hearing: Flaccus wanted to be a poet.

'Don't be afraid of Scylla and Charybdis,' Flaccus continued. *'The Sirens and the Harpies, and even the Cyclops hold no danger for you. You won't find such monsters, unless you erect altars to them in your heart.'*

Flavia didn't entirely understand the verses he had just recited, but there was something so profoundly beautiful about them that tears sprang to her eyes. She blinked them away angrily. How could someone so arrogant write such moving poetry?

'Always keep Ithaca in mind,' repeated Flaccus softly. *'Arriving there is what you are destined for.'*

At that moment he turned, and Flavia found herself staring straight into his dark eyes. It was obvious he had not expected to find anyone standing there because he turned away almost at once. But in that instant she had seen that his eyes were wet, too.

*

41

JUST AS THIS SHIP, OUR MOTHER, BORE US IN HER WOMB WITH MUCH GROANING, SO NOW WE MUST TAKE HER UPON OUR SHOULDERS AND BEAR HER ACROSS THIS COUNTRY OF SANDY WASTES.

'Excellent, Lupus,' said Aristo. 'Would you continue, Jonathan?'

'Why are we translating this passage?' sighed Flavia. 'If we're going to skip around can't we read a romantic part, like the one where Jason and Medea gaze into each other's eyes and fall in love?'

'I chose this passage for my last lesson with you because we're approaching the Isthmus of Corinth,' said Aristo. 'And we're about to carry the *Delphina* across dry land.'

Lupus and the others stared at him.

'Well it won't be us personally,' said Aristo with a laugh. 'We're not heroes like Jason and his argonauts. The *Delphina* will be carefully set on rollers and pulled along the *diolkos*.'

'Aren't we going to sail through the isthmus?' asked Flavia.

It was Aristo's turn to look puzzled.

'Sail,' repeated Flavia. 'You know: wind, sails, boat.' She gestured around her.

'We can't sail across the land.'

'No, I mean the isthmus. We'll sail through the isthmus.'

Aristo shook his head. 'The canal was never finished,' he said. 'Didn't you know that?'

'But pater always sails through the isthmus. He goes via the Isthmus of Corinth.'

'Of course he goes *via* the isthmus,' said Aristo, 'but

he goes over it, not through it. After Nero's death, work on the canal was abandoned. People still have to cross on land. Slaves pull the ships across on a kind of trolley.'

'Will you unembark at Corinth, Aristo?' asked Nubia.

'Yes. I'll disembark in Corinth.'

Lupus raised his eyebrows at Aristo to ask why.

'It's part of my contract with Flavia's father. Our agreement was that I teach Flavia – and the rest of you – for ten months of each year, and that I spend at least one month every year with my family. If the gods will it, you'll pick me up in a month or two, on your way back to Ostia.'

'How long does it take to cross the isthmus?' asked Jonathan.

'Only a day,' said Aristo. 'Unless there are lots of other ships ahead of us.'

Flavia tapped her stylus thoughtfully against her bottom teeth. 'Corinth will be our first chance to do some proper investigation. Maybe we can find out if the kidnapper's ship came this way.'

Lupus wrote on his wax tablet: HOW CAN WE FIND OUT?

'Good question,' said Jonathan. 'We don't even know the name of the ship that took Porcius and the rest.'

'The *Medea*,' said a low voice. Lupus looked up to see Bato standing behind them. 'The ship that took the children is called the *Medea*.'

SCROLL VII

'Why didn't you tell us about the *Medea* before?' Flavia asked Bato a few hours later. The four friends and Bato were walking across the scrubby soil of Greece towards some shaded taverns set back from the water's edge. Tigris raced ahead ecstatically, scattering lizards and barking at seagulls. They had stopped briefly in Lechaeum – Corinth's western port – to meet with the harbour-master and give thanks at the altar for a safe arrival. Then the *Delphina* had sailed a few miles further to reach the western end of the *diolkos*. Flavia's father had given her a handful of sesterces to buy everyone lunch.

'Keep your voices down,' whispered Bato, glancing back. Aristo, Flaccus and Zetes followed a few paces behind. 'I don't trust *anyone*.'

After five days at sea, Flavia felt the strange light-headedness that always came when she found herself on dry land after a sea voyage, as if she had drunk too much wine the night before. The scrubby ground jarred her feet and the air felt hot and heavy.

As they reached the tavern, Aristo and Flaccus chose a table in the sun but Flavia and her friends joined Bato at a shaded table beneath an awning of slatted reeds and grapevines.

Greece. She was in Greece. It was only a barren

stretch of warehouses and docks, but it was Greece! Flavia closed her eyes and inhaled. She could smell the faint scent of olive oil, sardines and wine. And there were other smells she couldn't identify. She savoured the delicious coolness of the shade on her skin and the coarse feel of the linen tablecloth under her forearms. When she opened her eyes, she had to squint against the dazzling light which bathed the scene. From here they could see the *Delphina*'s crew down on the quay-side, sweating in the hot sun as they unloaded the ship's cargo onto several ox carts. There were only two other ships in front of theirs, so the wait should not be long.

Flavia leaned closed to Bato. 'How did you know the name of the slave-ship?'

'I told you I visited Ostia's harbourmaster the day we left.' Bato looked at each of them with his pale eyes, 'He told me that *Medea* was the name of the ship that sailed without authorisation the day before.'

'Why didn't you tell us this earlier?' asked Flavia.

Bato sighed. 'The fewer people who know I know, the better. And I didn't want to involve you children.'

'Then why are you telling us now?' asked Jonathan, as Tigris flopped panting at his feet.

'Because now I need your help. After lunch I'm going to walk back to Lechaeum to speak to the harbour-master and see if the *Medea* has passed this way. I doubt she has, especially if she is carrying an illegal cargo of freeborn children. But I have to be sure. If she did not sail by way of the isthmus, she must have taken the longer and more dangerous route around Cape Malea.'

'Do you know where the *Medea* is going?'

'Rumour says Delos. But we can't be sure. That's where you can help me. Children can often go where

45

an adult can't. Go down to the *diolkos* after lunch and mingle with the workmen, officials and slaves. See if you can find out anything about slave-traders. You speak a little Greek, don't you?'

Flavia glanced at her friends. 'A little. And Lupus understands everything.'

'Good,' said Bato. 'Most Greeks like children. They won't mind you asking questions.'

He nodded towards the line of slaves and sailors taking goods off the *Delphina* in the shimmering heat. 'Your father and his men will be a couple of hours yet, so we have some time.'

'Why are you doing this?' asked Jonathan.

'What?' Bato looked surprised.

'You're not a magistrate any more. Why did you leave Ostia to come searching for kidnapped children?'

Bato sat back and shrugged. 'I have never hidden the fact that I want to climb the ladder of honours,' he said. 'As you know, magistrates are not allowed to hold the post for more than a year, nor are they allowed to hold office two years running. Next year I will run for a higher office. Meanwhile, during my year off I intend to make an impact, to do something special for Ostia. If I can restore freeborn children to their parents and break this slave-ring, I will earn the gratitude of many people.'

'You want to help stolen children?' asked Nubia. 'To bring them home?'

'That's right.' Bato leaned forward and lowered his voice. 'After Venalicius died, I wondered if the kidnappings would stop. If they did . . .' he broke off as a pretty serving-girl appeared before them. She placed a bowl of water under the table for Tigris, then stood and smiled down at them.

Bato said a few words to her in Greek, and she recited a list, obviously food, because Flavia caught the Greek words for olives and pistachio nuts.

'Try the stuffed vine leaves!' called Aristo from his sunny table. 'This place is famous for them.'

'We shall,' said Bato. When the girl had gone, he lowered his voice again. 'Where was I?'

'If the kidnappings stopped . . .' prompted Flavia.

'That's right. If the kidnappings stopped after the death of Venalicius, that would probably mean he had been running a private operation.'

'I think he was,' said Flavia. 'When we were in Surrentum after the volcano exploded, some men were taking kidnapped children to Venalicius. They called him "The Buyer".'

'Yes, I know about that,' said Bato. 'But there could have been someone even more senior than Venalicius.'

'You mean Venalicius might have had a buyer, too?' asked Jonathan.

'Exactly. Someone could have been supplying slaves to him, but then he sold them on to another slave-dealer, probably one with connections in Asia.'

'But the kidnappings *didn't* stop with the death of Venalicius,' said Flavia. 'They've started again.'

'Yes,' said Bato. 'As I see it, there are only two possibilities. The first is that this other buyer, let's call him Big Buyer, has appointed someone to take over Venalicius' area. The second possibility is that one of Venalicius' own men has decided to fill the vacancy left by his death. Either way,' said Bato, 'it appears as if the network is still operational, which makes me think—'

He stopped again as the girl set down a tray with two large copper beakers and five cups.

'There have long been rumours,' Bato continued a moment later, 'of a criminal mastermind running all the illegal slave-trade in the Empire.' He poured wine and water from the beakers into the ceramic cups.

'Is he Big Buyer?' asked Nubia.

'Perhaps. Or even someone above Big Buyer.'

'*Biggest* Buyer!' breathed Nubia.

Bato nodded grimly. 'We don't know much about this mastermind. Only conflicting rumours, the most curious of which is that he is a child.'

'A child?' Flavia's grey eyes were wide.

Bato grunted, added water to his wine and took a drink. 'But there are also rumours that he is a giant. And some say,' here he glanced at Lupus, 'some say he is mute. That his tongue has been cut out.'

Lupus coughed up the watered wine he had been tipping carefully down his throat. Nubia and Flavia patted him on the back.

'We don't even know where his base of operations is,' Bato continued, when Lupus had stopped coughing.

'How do we save the children if we don't know where he lives?' said Jonathan.

'Delos?' suggested Flavia. 'Isn't Delos the base for slave trade? Pater promised we could stop there to investigate.'

'I doubt it's the base of our mastermind,' said Bato. 'We can certainly look around, but Delos was the official centre for slave trade under the Republic. It's not much used any more. This man's base is probably further away. Perhaps on the coast of Asia, somewhere like Ephesus or Cnidos. Or it might be on one of the big islands: Rhodes, Cos or even Calymne.' He shrugged and took a sip of his wine. 'So far we don't have the faintest idea where he is. Or even who he is.'

'You don't know his name?' said Jonathan.

'No,' said Bato. 'Although he has several reported nicknames: Astyanax, Hector, Magnus, Minimus, even the Colossus.'

'Astyanax *and* Hector?' said Flavia. 'But how can that be? In *The Iliad*, Hector was Astyanax's father.'

'Does not Magnus mean "big",' said Nubia, 'and Minimus means "most small"?'

'And a colossus is a huge statue,' said Jonathan.

'I know,' admitted Bato with a sigh. 'It's a puzzle.'

'Wait!' hissed Flavia. 'Maybe it's a father and son team!'

Bato raised his eyebrows. 'That's one of my theories,' he said, and leaned forward again. 'Lupus, you told me once before about your uncle's last words. Remind me again?'

Lupus opened his wax tablet and began to write.

'They were in Greek,' said Flavia.

Lupus pushed the tablet forward. He had translated the words into Latin: PLEASE FORGIVE ME. HELP THE CHILDREN, THE ONES I TOOK.

'Anything else?' said Bato. 'Anything at all? You see, I believe that your uncle was one of the few people to know the identity of this criminal mastermind.'

'He did say one other thing,' offered Flavia. 'It was the last word he spoke.'

'It was the name of a girl,' said Nubia.

'Probably one of the ones who was kidnapped,' added Jonathan.

And Lupus held up his wax tablet with the girl's name in Latin: ROSA

Nubia held the pigeon gently in her hands, as Zosimus had taught her. They were standing on the flat roof of Helen's Hospitium, a luxury hotel in Cenchrea, the eastern port of Corinth. Dusk covered the sky like a gauzy pink veil and the cool breeze carried the scent of salt water and jasmine, and the distant sound of a donkey's bray. Slaves had pulled the *Delphina* on rollers across the four miles that separated the Ionian and Aegean Seas. Nubia and her friends had followed slowly on foot, chatting with sailors from other ships and those slaves who knew Latin. Jonathan had discovered that some of the slaves were Jewish, and had spoken to them in Aramaic. But nobody had heard of a ship called the *Medea*.

It was late afternoon by the time they arrived here at Cenchrea's best hotel, whose lovely owner Helen was known to Flavia's father. The crew had worked hard all day, and because they would have to repack the hold the following morning, Captain Geminus had decided to take them for a men's night out at the sanctuary of Aphrodite up on the Acrocorinth. Flaccus and Bato had gone, too. Only Zosimus had declined the invitation; he wanted to write a letter to his mother.

Nubia and her friends had made use of the famous baths-complex next door to the hotel, then dined with Helen in her private triclinium overlooking a herb garden. They had reached the dessert course when Nubia heard cooing pigeons passing on the other side of a box hedge. She had slipped away from the table to follow the sound, and now she stood on the hotel roof, her whole being focused on the pigeon in her hands.

'I think it is afraid,' she said. 'I can feel its heart beating fastly.'

'That's the normal speed for a bird's heart,' said Zosimus, his head bent over a square of papyrus and a piece of copper wire. 'You can tell he's not afraid because he's resting quietly.' He glanced up at her. 'You're very gentle. Animals can sense that. Even birds.'

'I love all animals,' said Nubia softly, 'except snakes.' The bird in her hands was surprisingly light and firm, like a warm, feather-covered gourd. It turned its head and regarded her with a bright ruby eye.

'Just keep holding him like that.' Zosimus was breathing heavily through his mouth as he rolled the tiny scrap of papyrus around a copper wire. 'So I can put this round his leg.'

'There you are, Nubia!' Flavia came up the white-washed stone steps onto the roof. 'What are you doing?'

'Look, Flavia!' Nubia held out the bird. 'His name is Achilles. Zosimus is sending a message to his mother in Ostia.'

'Ugh!' Flavia shuddered. 'I hate pigeons, with their horrible little red eyes and those legs like worms.'

'They're very useful creatures,' said Zosimus, pulling off his felt cap and stroking his short hair. 'Within a few hours, my mother will know that I have arrived safely in Corinth.'

'How?' asked Flavia.

'See that piece of papyrus around his leg? It's a letter to my mother.'

'Oh! I read about that in Pliny's *Natural History*!' said Flavia. 'He tells of people who use swallows to tell their friends which team won the races – by dipping their wings in the winning colour – and he talks about commanders sending written dispatches tied to pigeons' feet. But I've never seen anyone do it before.'

'What is your papyrus saying?' asked Nubia.

Zosimus replaced his cap. 'My old mother loves gossip. So I told her about our boy overboard, the Jewish boy with asthma and the two long-legged nymphs, one dark and one fair.' He winked at them. 'I've also written about our two highborn passengers and the beautiful slave-boy. And I always have to tell her what I've been eating. She worries about me, you see.'

Nubia felt her eyes grow wide. 'You write all those things on that most tiny piece of papyrus?'

Zosimus grinned. 'I write very small. You can let him go, now.'

'How?'

'Just like throwing a ball in the air.'

Nubia lifted her arms and tossed the pigeon up, releasing the feathered body into the evening air and laughing as its beating wings made a breeze on her face.

'Go with Hermes!' cried Zosimus.

Flavia squealed, covering her head with her hands, but her face broke into a smile as the pigeon flew up and then wheeled away to the east, where a star already burned in the darkening violet sky.

Nubia frowned. 'Isn't Ostia that way?' She pointed towards the setting sun.

'Of course.' Zosimus chuckled. 'Achilles has to have a good look around before he gets his bearings.'

'Oh,' said Nubia, 'But how does he know where to go?'

Zosimus patted the wicker cage full of cooing

pigeons. 'Every one of these beauties was born and raised in Ostia, in the dovecote of my mother's house. No matter how far away I take them, they can always find their way back to that dovecote.' He stood up and smiled at them. 'But don't ask me how they do it. That's a mystery.'

In the darkest hour of the night, Flavia Gemina sat up in her bed in an upper room of Helen's Hospitium.

'Of course!' she cried. 'I'm an idiot!'

'I agree,' mumbled Jonathan from a bed across the room. 'Only an idiot would get up in the middle of the night. Go back to sleep.'

Flavia ignored him. 'Lupus!' she hissed. 'Wake up!'

Translucent geckos scuttled across the red and black panels of the frescoed wall as Flavia took her small bronze night-lamp over to a standing candelabra in the middle of the room. When she had lit all ten wicks, she perched on Lupus's bed and reached for his wax tablet. At the foot of Jonathan's bed, Tigris raised his head and thumped his tail.

'Lupus,' she said. 'Venalicius spoke his last words in Greek. Today you translated them into Latin. Can you write down exactly what he wrote? But this time in Greek?'

Lupus yawned, then nodded, his eyes very green in the yellow lamplight. He sat up, took the wax tablet and thought for a moment. Then he began to write. The bed creaked as Nubia came to sit beside Flavia. Tigris pushed his cold nose against Flavia's knee, and Jonathan came over, his shadow flickering on the red and black wall.

They all watched as Lupus wrote in Greek.

53

'Don't forget the last word he spoke,' whispered Flavia. 'The girl's name.'

Lupus suddenly gripped her arm, and she saw understanding in his eyes.

'Yes!' she whispered. 'He wasn't trying to tell us *who*, but *where*!'

POΔON wrote Lupus.

'*Eis Rhodon*,' whispered Flavia in Greek. 'He was trying to say "*eis Rhodon*"!'

And Jonathan translated: 'To Rhodes.'

SCROLL VIII

'Rhodes?' said Bato the next morning at breakfast. 'Are you sure?'

They were all sitting in the cool morning courtyard of the hotel, eating a breakfast of olives, cheese and sesame rolls with honey. Below the table, brown hens pecked at the crumbs, and from somewhere nearby came the raucous crow of a rooster.

'Yes,' said Flavia. 'It's a girl's name but in Greek it's also the name of the island. It fits all the facts, and it even explains one of the Big Buyer's nicknames.'

'Of course!' said Bato. 'The Colossus . . . The Colossus of Rhodes!'

'What about the Colossus of Rhodes?' said a deep voice.

Flavia looked up to see Flaccus coming towards their table. He was wearing a clean tunic and his dark hair was damp. Zetes – his golden hair also damp – pulled back a chair for his master but remained standing.

'What about the Colossus?' repeated Flaccus, taking a plate and a sesame roll.

'It's one of the Seven Sights!' said Flavia, thinking fast. 'You wanted to see the Seven Sights and . . . that's one of them.'

'So is Rhodes our new destination?' Flaccus grasped a

55

handful of olives, dropped them on his plate and wiped his fingers on Zetes's tunic. 'I thought we were heading for Delos.'

'We'll stop at Delos,' said Flavia. 'But then I think pater wants to go to Rhodes to get some . . . um . . . Rhodian things.' She caught a whiff of the musky cinnamon-scented oil which Flaccus had rubbed on his body. 'Scented oil,' she said. 'Rose-scented oil. The island of Rhodes is famous for its roses. They should all be in bloom now.'

'And hardbake,' said Bato, biting into a soft sesame roll.

'What?' said Flavia.

'Rhodian hardbake. It's a kind of bread, but rock hard. Also oil flasks,' he added. 'Rhodes is famous for its oil flasks. I have one at home in the shape of a warrior's helmet.'

'And chickens,' said Jonathan as the cock crowed again. 'The . . . er . . . famous chickens of Rhodes.'

'That's right,' said Bato. 'Rhodes breeds some of the fiercest fighting cocks.'

Jonathan looked surprised, but Flaccus did not seem to notice. He was staring at the bronze charm that Flavia was absent-mindedly fingering. When she saw the direction of his gaze she blushed furiously and dropped the amulet back under the neck of her tunic.

And for the first time in a week, Gaius Valerius Flaccus smiled at her.

After the crew had finished repacking the *Delphina*'s hold, Captain Geminus sacrificed a sheep at the Temple of Poseidon in Corinth, asking the god of the sea to give them a good voyage.

Their prayers seemed to have been answered, for as they left Cenchrea, a wind rose from the west. It was a strong warm breeze which filled the dolphin sail with a delicious urgency and gave the *Delphina*'s prow a white moustache as she sped across the dark blue Aegean. Flavia's father called it *Zephyrus*, and he explained that such a following wind meant Jove was in a good mood.

Because the *Medea* had not been sighted at Corinth, they knew it must have taken the longer southern route. They might catch up with the slave-ship at Delos, but for the next two or three days there was no point even looking out for it.

They had said their goodbyes to Aristo in Lechaeum and promised him that they would spend a few hours every morning studying the *Argonautica*. But because the Greek version was too difficult to tackle without his help, Flavia and Jonathan took turns reading Varro's Latin translation out loud. When Zetes wasn't shaving his master or washing or mending, he would join them and listen with open-mouthed attention.

After their morning reading, Flavia wrote in her diary, Jonathan did his exercises, Nubia helped feed the pigeons, and Lupus helped the crew. Flavia knew Lupus was trying to learn the ropes so that he could be a good captain. Bato and Flaccus spent their time discussing politics and philosophy at the stern platform, which had become their area of the ship. Flavia was pleased that although they were of the patrician class and her father only an equestrian, they often included him in their conversations.

After lunch, Flavia would read and Nubia would play her flute. Lupus and Jonathan practised archery, shooting at a knot-hole near the top of the foremast, but they lost too many arrows overboard, so they abandoned bow and arrows for their slings. Oyster shells were their ammunition and seagulls their targets. Zetes occasionally joined them, if he was not attending his master.

Like Jove, Captain Geminus was in a benevolent mood and sometimes he let them play hide-and-seek with Tigris. One of them would hide – usually Lupus – and the others would take Tigris into the deckhouse and count to a hundred. Then they would let Tigris out with a cry of: 'Where's Lupus, Tigris? Where's Lupus?' Tigris would race around the ship in his search for Lupus. Finally his deep regular barks told them where Lupus was hiding.

Jonathan's dog had now become an accepted member of the crew. He was used to the constantly moving deck and he kept out of the way. At dinner he sat under the table where the sailors would ruffle his fur affectionately and give him scraps to eat.

Dinner was Flavia's favourite time of the day. She knew that on most ships the passengers were expected to provide their own food, and that they rarely ate with the crew. But on board the *Delphina*, everybody ate together. That meant she could position herself next to the youngest crew member, Silvanus. Or better yet, across from him. He had long-lashed green eyes and a flashing smile. And his hair smelled faintly of lavender.

After Corinth, Flaccus allowed Zetes to sit, rather than make him be the only one standing throughout the meal, so sometimes Flavia found herself seated opposite the two most beautiful boys she had ever seen.

The grey-haired sailor called Atticus had proved to be a skilled cook. Every night he brought out a big bowl of stew which everyone scooped up with flat bread bought at their most recent port. They had finished the beef, but now there was mutton left over from their sacrifice at Corinth, and Atticus varied it with fish stew on alternate days.

They ate dinner in the shelter of a port, or anchored in a secluded cove, and twice they docked early enough to visit the baths first, once on Cythnos and once on Syros.

After sunset, during that magical hour of twilight, they would sit around the long table to drink pine-scented wine and eat honeyed sweets and talk or play music. Flavia's father told stories which Flavia had never heard before. Flaccus could recite whole tracts of Homer's *Iliad* in Latin, but more often they asked for passages from his poem, a reworking of the *Odyssey*. The verses still made Flavia shiver and aroused a strange confusion in her. When Flaccus recited these verses with his soft voice she could almost love him. But a moment later he would do something to make her hate him again: he would look right through her or chomp his gum like a cow.

Zetes was only a slave, but he played the buzzy double aulos superbly. Flaccus strummed the lyre, and although he was not as good as Aristo, his singing voice was as deep and soft as rabbit's fur. When Flaccus and Zetes played together it sent shivers down Flavia's spine. When she and her friends played music in their turn, Flavia could tell the others were impressed.

Finally, when it was too dark to see each other's expressions, Punicus would light the night-lamps and they would retire to their hammocks or sheepskins. Since Nubia's first restless night, all four friends had slept together up on deck, in the sheltered 'V' of the prow. Flavia's father and one of the crew also slept up on deck, but the other crew members, the two passengers and Zetes slept in hammocks below.

After a third day of perfect sailing, as Flavia lay on her sheepskin and gazed up at the star-filled sky, with music still ringing in her head, she realised there had been no accidents or bad omens since they had left Corinth.

'Maybe,' she thought, as she drifted off, 'maybe Fortuna is smiling on us at last. Maybe we'll catch up with the *Medea* at Delos and save all the children.'

Despite their hopes, an afternoon's exploration showed them that there was no slave trade on Delos, and no ship named the *Medea* had ever dropped anchor there.

As the *Delphina* left the tiny island in its wake and sailed on through the golden light of late afternoon, Jonathan finally achieved the task he had set himself ten days before. He pulled himself up the rope all the way to the top of the mast.

He ignored a smattering of good-natured applause from the deck below and tried to keep his face straight. But he was still smiling when he jumped back down onto the deck. He had done it. He had accomplished something he had set his mind to.

'Very good,' said Flaccus, folding his own muscular arms. 'Your self-discipline is admirable. And I applaud the fact that you haven't allowed your asthma to be a handicap.'

Jonathan nodded politely. A few steps took him to the wooden rod which held the awning in front of the deckhouse. Ignoring the ache in his left shoulder, he gripped this bar underhanded, and started to do his pull-ups.

Flaccus followed him. 'I've been watching you,' he said. 'And if I didn't know better I'd say you'd trained in a gladiator school.'

'What makes you . . . say that?' Jonathan grunted between pull-ups.

'My old boxing teacher was a gladiator,' said Flaccus. 'He taught me those exercises. And a few others.'

Jonathan lowered himself from the bar and turned to face Flaccus.

'You know how to box?'

'I do.'

'Will you teach me?'

Flaccus raised a dark eyebrow and gave Jonathan a half smile. 'It's a brutal sport. And once I've taught you, your fists will be deadly weapons. Are you sure you want to learn?'

'Yes,' said Jonathan without hesitation. 'Oh, yes.'

'Watch out, Lupus!' screamed Flavia Gemina a few moments later. 'One false move and you're dead!'

Lupus scowled, his hand hovering over the wooden game board. Finally he moved one of the bone discs.

'Wrong move,' said Bato with a chuckle, moving his ebony counter to take Lupus's piece. 'I win.'

Lupus sighed as Bato chalked his twelfth win onto the hatch-cover beside them. He wished Bato hadn't found out about his special dice. He was much better at games when he could cheat.

'Watch out, Lupus!' Flavia screamed again.

Again Lupus glared at her but this time he saw her horrified upturned face and heard the creak of ropes from above. He looked up just in time to see the *Delphina*'s massive yard-arm plunging straight towards him.

SCROLL IX

The yard struck the *Delphina*'s long table with a resounding boom which made the whole boat shudder, and as the echo died away Jonathan heard the sound of the sail crumpling to the deck, like the collapsing wings of a giant wounded bird.

'Lupus!' Jonathan ran forward from the stern where he had been practising boxing moves with Flaccus.

'He's all right!' cried Flavia's father, helping Lupus out from under the folds of heavy linen. 'But Bato's pinned down. I need help. Zosimus! Atticus!'

But Flaccus was already there. His biceps bulged as he strained to lift the heavy yard-arm. Jonathan moved to help him and together they lifted the heavy beam long enough for Captain Geminus to disappear back underneath the sailcloth. A moment later he emerged with his arm around a white-faced Bato.

Jonathan saw that Bato's right arm hung limply and that it seemed too long for his body. 'I think you've dislocated your shoulder,' he said. 'Does it hurt?'

Bato nodded. Then he fainted into the captain's arms.

Nubia held the steaming beaker and hesitated as Flavia disappeared down the wooden hatch steps into the shadowy hold of the ship. Every time she descended she felt the ghostly clamp of cold iron around her neck and the memories came rushing up.

But they needed the drink she and Flavia had prepared, so she took a deep breath and went down.

'Will he be all right?' she heard Flavia ask as she reached the bottom step.

Nubia gripped the rail with her left hand, and as her eyes adjusted she saw that Bato was not in his hammock, but stretched out on a firm bag of salt beneath it. He was pale but conscious, with Lupus on one side and Jonathan on the other.

'He'll be fine,' said Jonathan. 'Lupus helped me pull his shoulder back into place while he was unconscious. The arm was only dislocated, not broken. I've helped Father do it once or twice.'

'Just as well I fainted,' said Bato, giving Jonathan a weak smile.

'And just as well Jonathan brought his father's spare herb pouch,' said Flavia. 'Nubia and I made you a cup of hot spiced wine with poppy tears.'

Jonathan nodded. 'I gave them the recipe. It will ease the pain and help you sleep.'

The *Delphina* was running smoothly again, but Nubia stepped carefully on the firm bags of salt so that she wouldn't spill the potion. She knelt and helped Bato drink.

'Thank you,' he said a moment later, letting his head sink back onto a pillow made from a folded cloak. 'That's wonderful.'

Flavia sat beside Bato and whispered. 'Pater just told me there's no way that yard could have fallen by itself.

Someone loosened the knots of a rope at the very back of the ship.'

Lupus wrote: HALYARD

'Someone tries to hurt us?' Nubia's hand went automatically to her throat.

Flavia nodded. 'It was no accident. The ship's not evil and the gods aren't angry. I should have thought of this earlier. Someone on this ship is trying to thwart our mission.'

'I was afraid of this,' said Bato, looking at them with his pale eyes. 'We have an enemy on board.'

Flavia nodded. 'Probably an agent of the Big Buyer.'

'Who do you think it is?' asked Jonathan.

Flavia glanced around the dim hold, them lowered her voice. 'Pater said that anybody who knows about ships could have untied the knot and then moved away. It wouldn't fall straight away if the knot was just loosened.'

'So that means it could be anyone on board this ship,' said Bato.

'Not Flaccus,' said Jonathan. 'He's not a sailor.'

'But he might know about ships,' said Flavia. 'And I haven't trusted him from the first moment I saw him.'

'Shall I ask him if he knows anything about ships?' said Jonathan.

'You can't just ask him directly. He'll guess that we suspect him.' Flavia thoughtfully sucked a strand of hair that had come unpinned. 'Eureka!' she said a moment later. 'I've got a plan to find out if Flaccus knows the ropes.'

THEY SET UP THE TALL MAST IN ITS MASTBOX AND SECURED IT WITH FORESTAYS PULLED

TIGHT ON EACH SIDE. THEN THEY LET DOWN
THE SAIL FROM THE YARD-ARM AND FASTENED
THE HALYARD TO THE DECK, ROUND ITS OWN
WELL POLISHED PIN

'Very good, Lupus,' said Gaius Valerius Flaccus
between chomps of his gum. 'That's an extremely
competent translation.' The sun was low in the sky,
shining red through a haze above the horizon. Its light
gave Flaccus's straight hair deep mahogany highlights
as he bent over the scroll.

'Thank you for helping us with this part of the *Argonautica*,' said Flavia to Flaccus with a sweet smile. 'But
I'm confused. Can you tell me the difference between a
forestay and a halyard?'

'Well,' said Flaccus, flicking his hair away from his
face. 'Do you see those two big ropes running from the
mast to the very front of the ship, the prow?'

'Yes.'

'Those are the forestays. They hold up the mast.'

'Is not the mast being stuck to the ship with big
nails?' asked Nubia.

'No. You need to be able to adjust its angle.' Flaccus
held up his forearm to demonstrate.

'Why doesn't the little mast at the front have ropes?'
asked Flavia.

'Unlike the mainmast, the foremast *is* fixed to the
hull, so it doesn't need ropes to hold it up.' He got up
from the bench and gestured for them to follow him to
the other side of the sail. 'Now, do you see those four
heavy ropes which come down on either side of the
mainmast? The ones Jonathan has been climbing?
Those are called stays. They prevent the mast from
falling to one side or the other.'

Jonathan pointed to half a dozen short ropes above the sail. 'What about those little ropes up there, going from the top of the mast down to the yard-arm?'

'What is yard-arm?' asked Nubia.

'It's that lying-down piece of wood,' said Flavia. 'The one that fell down an hour ago.'

Flaccus nodded and cracked his gum. 'That's right. The yard is the cross-beam from which the sail hangs.'

Flavia looked at the back of the sail, blood-red in the light of the sinking sun, and she shivered.

Flaccus continued, 'And those short ropes Jonathan was asking about are called lifts. They hold the yard-arm in place. They're attached to the halyard at that discus-shaped fitting near the top of the mast.'

Nubia pointed. 'So that big rope there is called halyard?'

Flaccus squinted at the rope, then nodded. 'Yes. It's attached to a brass pin near the back of the ship.'

'What would happen if you were to untie it?' Flavia asked him.

Flaccus stopped chewing and held her gaze with his dark eyes. 'Then the yard-arm would fall down,' he said, 'exactly as it did today.'

'I'm sure Floppy is the agent,' whispered Flavia later that night. The four of them were wrapped in their fleeces in the shelter of the prow. 'It was the way he looked at me with those beady eyes of his.'

'You just don't like him,' said Jonathan, 'but I do. And I think it's much more likely that our culprit is one of the crew.'

Flavia sighed. 'All right,' she said, 'I suppose we

should interrogate the crew. We'll do it first thing tomorrow morning, using the Nubia-method.'

Lupus gave his 'huh?' grunt.

'That's where you go up to someone but don't say very much. The awkward silence sometimes makes the person blurt out the truth.'

'Interesting,' said Jonathan. 'I'll try the Nubia-method on Atticus.'

'I will try the Nubia-method on Zosimus,' said Nubia. 'While I help him send a pigeon-letter.'

'Good,' said Flavia. 'I'll interview Silvanus. I have a feeling about him.'

Jonathan snorted. 'I think you have a feeling *for* him.'

Flavia ignored this last comment. 'Lupus, can you interrogate Punicus?'

Lupus grunted yes.

'Good,' said Flavia. 'But everybody keep an eye on Floppy. I still think he's the one who's trying to stop us.'

'Myconos,' said Silvanus to Flavia the next morning after breakfast. He had just sluiced the deck with a bucket of seawater and now he was arranging a length of rope in a spiral on its damp surface. 'This island is Myconos. They call it the island of bald men. At least that's what Atticus says. Zosimus says if I set foot on land I'll lose all my hair.'

'They were probably teasing you,' said Flavia, gazing at his wavy black hair and wondering what it would feel like to run her fingers through it. 'I don't think you have to worry about going bald yet. How old are you?' she asked, forgetting to use the Nubia-method.

He glanced up at her with his long-lashed green eyes, 'I'll be seventeen next month.'

Flavia gazed at him for a while, then remembered she was supposed to be questioning him. 'Um . . . do you like being a sailor?'

'Not really. I'd rather be a baker or a tavern-owner. I don't think I'm very good at this. I almost killed poor Lupus last week.'

'What exactly happened?'

'I was supposed to be knotting or splicing or . . . something, and the rope was slippery. It just whipped out of my hand. That was when the wind caught the sail and jerked the boat and Lupus fell out. I'm not a sailor. The only thing I'm good at is arranging the rope in a pretty design like this. I'd much rather have my feet on solid ground.'

'Why are you here, then?' asked Flavia.

'A girl.'

Flavia's heart thudded. 'You're . . . There's a girl you like? On board this ship?'

He flushed. 'In Ostia. Her name is Titia,' he said softly. 'She's not what you might call beautiful. She's cross-eyed. But she's got a lovely—'

'Titia? The baker's daughter?'

'That's the one.' His flush deepened.

'But she's Porcius's sister!'

'I know,' he said in a low voice. 'That's why I signed up for this cruise. I know the real reason for this voyage. I know you want to find the kidnapped children.'

'How did you . . . What makes you think that?'

'Everybody knows it,' he said, looking up at her from beneath his straight dark eyebrows. 'In a town as small as Ostia you can't keep much hidden.'

'You mean you knew before we even set sail?' said Flavia.

Silvanus nodded. 'Everybody knows how you and your friends killed that monster Venalicius, and that you're trying to find the kidnapped children.'

Flavia opened her mouth to protest, then shut it again.

'Titia knew her brother wouldn't just run off and leave his pet mice behind,' said Silvanus. 'She suspected kidnappers. I thought that if I could find Porcius and save him, she'd be so grateful that . . . She doesn't love me, you see. She loves someone else.'

'Why didn't you tell us you wanted to find the kidnapped children, too?'

He shrugged. 'I don't know. You're all so clever and highborn. I'm just a pleb.'

'But that's silly, Nubia and Lupus aren't highborn and they – oh never mind!' Flavia sighed, then lowered her voice. 'Silvanus, have you noticed anyone acting suspiciously during this voyage? Especially just before the accidents occur? Flaccus maybe?'

'I don't know. It's all so new to me. But there are a few things that seem strange—'

'Silvanus!' called Flavia's father from the hatchway. 'Will you go into town with Zosimus and get some water and bread? I want to weigh anchor within the next hour or two.'

'Yes, sir!' said Silvanus, and turned back to Flavia, 'One of the things that's been bothering me,' he whispered, 'is how sometimes the ropes are dry and sometimes they're slippery, almost oily. I think—'

'Silvanus!' Her father's voice. 'Now!'

Silvanus touched Flavia lightly on the arm. 'I'll tell you later,' he said, with a heart-stopping smile. 'As soon as I get back.'

SCROLL X

Lupus saw the sea urchins as the sun rose behind the town wall and slanted its golden shafts into the water.

Dozens of them clung to the rocks below the jetty, just under the surface, as spiky as horse-chestnut seed cases and as brown as the nut inside. He ran below, found his net and went back up onto the deck.

Then, stripping off his tunic, he plunged into the water.

By the gods it was cold! This was not the mild Tyrrhenian Sea, warmed by months of summer sun or heated by sulphurous steam, but the Aegean after an unusually cold winter.

But soon his body grew used to the cold. Urchins had been his father's favourite dish and he faintly remembered their sweet chewy taste. He might not be able to enjoy them, but his friends could. Although the urchins had wicked spikes, they came away from the rocks easily; he only pricked himself once.

After old Atticus helped him back onto the deck Lupus put on his tunic and sucked his wounded finger. He spat out the poison and shook his hand, but the finger still hurt like Hades.

'Do you know how to make the stinging stop?' Atticus stroked his woolly grey hair and grinned.

Lupus nodded and went to the rail. There he turned his back to his friends, lifted his tunic and urinated on his finger, making sure that the rising breeze was behind him.

'Ewww! Lupus!' cried Flavia. 'What are you doing?'

'It's the only way.' Atticus chuckled and lifted the dripping net full of urchins from a puddle on the deck. 'Oh, Lupus, these are lovely! At least three dozen here. This will make us a tasty first course for our dinner tonight,' he added, and disappeared towards the deck-house.

Lupus turned and grinned at his friends.

But his grin faded when he saw the expression on Bato's face. Ostia's junior magistrate had just jumped off the gangplank onto the deck and was gripping Captain Geminus's arm.

'Captain!' hissed Bato. 'I just spoke to some fisherman who saw a ship called the *Medea* leaving early this morning. They said she was heading south. If we hurry, we might catch her before she reaches Rhodes.'

'Great Neptune's beard! Where is Silvanus?' asked Flavia's father angrily. 'The harbourmaster tells me this breeze only lasts until noon, and sometimes not even that long. Punicus! Atticus! Zosimus!'

'Yes, sir?' Punicus and Zosimus looked up from polishing the rail and Atticus appeared in the deckhouse door, wearing a leather apron and heavy canvas gloves. He'd been preparing the sea urchins and held a mallet in one of his gloved hands.

'Where is Silvanus?' repeated Captain Geminus.

They all looked at one another. Then Zosimus put down his cloth and stepped forward.

'Silvanus and me went into town together about an hour ago, rolling the empty water barrel between us. But we parted ways at the main square. I left him at the fountain and went to the baker's. I brought the loaves back here and when I went back to the fountain Silvanus and the barrel were gone. I reckoned he got some local boys to help him roll it back. I never knew he wasn't back until now.'

'Jupiter blast it! Atticus! Zosimus! You speak Greek. See if you can find him. We're sailing at noon and if he's not back by then, we'll have to sail without him.'

'Can we help them look for Silvanus?' cried Flavia, her heart thumping. 'Something must have happened to him.'

Her father hesitated, then nodded. 'Very well. Take Tigris with you and stay together. And promise me,' he added, 'that you'll be back before noon.'

Early that afternoon, Lupus found his friends sitting beside the crate of cooing pigeons in the V of the *Delphina*'s prow. He hadn't tricked Punicus into blurting out a confession, but the helmsman had given him an old papyrus chart of the islands and Lupus had made an exciting discovery. His smile faded when he saw that Flavia's head was bowed and Nubia was patting her back.

'Flavia's upset because we didn't wait for Silvanus,' said Jonathan, who was sitting beside the girls.

'Pater makes me so angry sometimes!' said Flavia, raising her tear-stained face from her hands. 'Silvanus was about to give us some vital clues. And I know he would have been on our side. Remember Porcius's older sister Titia? The one with the cross-eyes?'

'The one who is loving Aristo?' asked Nubia.

'Yes. Silvanus loves her and he would have done anything to help us find Porcius. But now pater has left him behind on that island—'

'Myconos,' said Jonathan.

Lupus grunted and unrolled his papyrus chart and spread it on the moving deck. He pointed to the island labelled MYCONOS.

'—and he didn't give us enough time to look for him!'

'But the wind might have died, Flavia,' said Jonathan. 'Your father made the only decision he could. If we hadn't left at noon we wouldn't have caught this breeze and we might have lost a whole day's travel. We all want to catch the *Medea*.'

Nubia nodded. 'Saving the children is most important,' she said.

Lupus rattled the papyrus and when he had their attention he moved his finger along the map towards its lower right hand corner.

'Yes,' said Flavia, wiping her nose on her arm, 'that's the route the *Medea* will probably take.'

Lupus made his finger pass between various islands, but just before he reached Rhodes, his finger stopped and he jabbed at the papyrus chart. Between two peninsulas jutting out from the mainland labelled CARIA was a little island about the same size as Myconos.

Nubia read the letters slowly: 'SYMI,' she read, and then: 'Symi!'

Lupus nodded, his eyes bright with excitement.

'Didn't you know that, Lupus?' said Flavia. 'Didn't you realise that Symi is right next to Rhodes?'

Lupus shook his head and pulled out his wax tablet:

WE COULD BE THERE TOMORROW he wrote.

'But Lupus,' said Jonathan. 'If we stop at Symi we may never catch the slave-ship *Medea*.'

'We must save the children first,' said Nubia.

Flavia nodded. 'They're right, Lupus. We've got to save the children first. *Then* you can go to Symi.'

Lupus stared at Flavia open-mouthed. A moment earlier she had been sobbing about Silvanus, a pretty-boy she barely knew. Now she was telling him he couldn't take a few hours to try to find out if his own mother was still alive.

He stood up, uttered a cry of rage and threw down his wax tablet and stylus. Nubia cried out and as Lupus turned he realised the stylus had bounced on the deck and struck her forearm. But he didn't stop. He had to get away. He had to be alone.

A rapid glance around showed him Zosimus up in the rigging as usual, Atticus in the deckhouse doorway, Punicus and Captain Geminus at the tiller. Flaccus and his slave-boy were probably below with Bato. Where could he go to be alone on board a small ship?

Suddenly he knew.

Lupus ran across the rolling deck and up the stairs to the *Delphina*'s stern platform. Ignoring the cries of his friends, he climbed over the rail at the back of the ship and dropped out of sight.

Lupus crouched in the skiff, breathing hard, every muscle in his body clenched with rage. He had his back to the *Delphina* because he didn't want to see the others looking down on him from their superior position. He hated them.

He hated Flavia, who had been sobbing her heart out

74

a few moments earlier because she couldn't find the latest object of her desire. Flavia whose eyes were still red and swollen as she told him that he couldn't take one day to try to find his mother.

He hated Jonathan, too, whose mother had returned to him and who covered him with kisses and wept when he left.

He even hated Nubia. He hated her because she was so gentle and perfect and never lost her temper. And because even though the stylus had made her bleed, she only looked at him with understanding in her eyes, not anger.

He hated them all. He hated them because they could talk and taste food and lick their lips and drink water without choking. He hated them because they had tongues while he had only a stump. Like an animal. No. Worse than an animal. Even animals had tongues.

He tried to remember the time when he had still had a tongue. When he had been happy. Before he had known pain or fear. He closed his eyes and saw himself running on a smooth golden beach, playing ball with the children of Symi. He saw himself swimming in that silent blue-green world of fish and coral and silver bubbles. He saw his father, strong and tanned, sitting in a skiff like this one and laughing with his white teeth. He remembered his mother's soft voice, and the refrain of a lullaby she had used to sing: *When you come home, when you come home to me.*

In his mind's eye he saw her from behind, her honey-coloured hair screening her face as she set food on a table in the shelter of a grapevine. Lupus tried to make her turn around in his imagination. But she wouldn't and he realised with a stab of grief that he could no longer remember what she looked like. He could not remember his own mother's face.

Lupus opened his tongueless mouth and tried to call her, but the only sound which emerged was a strangled howl. How would he find her again if he could not even recognise her? Now he would always be alone. Alone and unloved.

He couldn't stop the great tearing sobs which began to shake his whole body. So he surrendered himself to grief and as he wept he felt the hot tears dissolve his anger.

Presently, rocked by the dark blue waves of the Aegean, Lupus fell asleep.

Nubia was examining the cut on her arm when a shadow fell across her. She looked up to see Flaccus standing over her. The sun was behind his head so she couldn't see his expression clearly. But his deep voice seemed kind.

'You're hurt. What happened?'

'Lupus throws down stylus and it strikes me. Flavia and Jonathan go down to find ointment.'

'Here,' he said, squatting down beside her and taking a handkerchief out of his belt pouch. 'Let's stop the bleeding at least.'

He gently tied the cloth round her arm and glanced towards the back of the ship.

'I saw Lupus go down into the skiff. Bato tells me the reason he's as quiet as Telephus is because his tongue was cut out. Is that true?'

'Yes, it is true. Lupus is only six years old when he sees his father being murdered by a bad man. The bad man cuts out the tongue of Lupus so he cannot inform.'

'By Hercules!' Flaccus sat cross-legged on the sun-warmed deck beside her. 'Poor lad. I know what it's like to have a disability,' he said, 'though mine's nowhere near as bad.'

'A what?'

'Nothing.' He took some ivory-coloured nuggets from his belt pouch and popped one in his mouth. He held the rest out to her. 'Have some gum. It's nice.'

'Thank you,' said Nubia, and took four pieces.

'And you?' he asked. 'How do you come to be in Rome? Or rather on a Roman ship?'

'Last year,' said Nubia, 'some bad men come to my tents at night. They kill my father and put the rest of my clan in chains. They take us to a town called Alexandria and there they sell us to the bad man who killed Lupus's father. He is being a slave-dealer with one eye.'

'The same man who cut out Lupus's tongue?' Flaccus raised his eyebrows.

'Yes.'

'He should die.'

'He is die.'

'I thought you said he is a slave-dealer.'

'I am still learning Latin,' said Nubia. 'Sometimes it is hard to find the right words for time. I am sorry.'

'No, no,' he said, chewing his gum. 'You speak very well for someone who's been learning the language for less than a year.'

'Thank you. Flavia teaches me Latin by reading to me the *Aeneid*.'

'Oh?'

Nubia nodded. 'She buys me for a slave and then sets me free. Flavia is very kind.'

'Is she?' he said, flicking dark hair from his eyes and

cracking his gum. 'To me she seems like a bossy little domina. I pity the man she marries.'

Nubia felt her face grow warm and she kept her eyes on the deck.

'And here she comes now,' said Flaccus, rising to his feet. 'So I'm off.' He looked down at her and said quietly, 'The Cyclops will hold no danger for you, Nubia, unless you erect an altar to him in your heart.'

Flavia narrowed her eyes at Flaccus's retreating back.

'Was Floppy bothering you, Nubia?'

Nubia shook her head. 'No. He gives me his hand-kerchief.' She held out her arm.

'Ugh!' Flavia shuddered. 'It probably had patrician snot on it.'

Jonathan laughed and sat beside Nubia. 'Take it off for a moment,' he said, 'so I can put some balm on the cut.'

Nubia obediently pulled back Flaccus's handkerchief.

'It's not too bad,' said Jonathan, examining her fore-arm. He lifted the lid from a tiny round ceramic pot, dipped his finger in the ointment and gently dabbed it on the cut.

'He also gives me gum.'

'Oh! Let's see!' cried Flavia.

Nubia held out her palm. On it were four little chunks of ivory-coloured resin.

'You got a piece for Lupus,' said Jonathan, taking one.

'Yes,' said Nubia. 'So he does not feel forsaken. Shall we call him?'

'No,' said Jonathan. 'Let's give him time to calm down. He'll come back when he's ready.'

'Lupus will come to his senses eventually,' said Flavia, also taking a nugget from Nubia's hand. 'He'll realise he can go and look for his mother after we've saved the children.'

'I think it's mastic,' said Jonathan, putting the gum in his mouth. 'My father sometimes prescribes it for bad breath and also for stomach pains. I've never tried it.'

'Hey!' said Flavia. 'That must be where we get the word "masticate". Because you chew it.'

The three of them chewed thoughtfully for a moment.

'Mmmm,' said Flavia. 'It tastes a bit like carrot, only sweeter.'

'A bit like aniseed,' said Nubia.

'And cumin,' said Jonathan.

Flavia took hers out of her mouth and examined it. 'Look! It's turned white.'

'Do you swallow it like food?' asked Nubia.

'I don't think so,' said Jonathan and added, 'You know, I have an idea about the mysterious disappearance of Silvanus.'

'What?' said Flavia.

Jonathan looked at her, chewing thoughtfully, then shook his head. 'No, it's stupid. It's crazy.'

'What?' said Flavia. 'Tell us!'

'Remember we made a list matching the people on board this ship with the heroes on Jason's voyage? And we said Silvanus was like Hylas?'

'Yes.'

'Well, don't you think it's strange that Silvanus disappeared just like Hylas, while going for water?'

Flavia stopped chewing her gum and stared at him.

Jonathan shrugged. 'I told you it was a stupid theory,' he said.

'No, Jonathan. It's not stupid at all.'

'It is prickly,' whispered Nubia.

'What?' said Jonathan.

'It causes my neck hairs to be prickly,' said Nubia, making the sign against evil.

'Someone,' said Flavia, 'must have overheard us assigning roles to the passengers and crew.'

'Unless they read it,' said Jonathan. 'Aristo had you ink it on the back of your tablet.'

'That's right.' Flavia took out her wax tablet. 'So whoever got rid of Silvanus can probably read and write. That eliminates Atticus straightaway; he can't read. But Zosimus and Punicus can.' She narrowed her eyes. 'And so can Floppy.'

'Also Zetes,' said Nubia. 'I hear him reading from a scroll to Floppy yesterday.'

Jonathan pointed to the list written in ink on the wooden back of Flavia's tablet. 'Uh-oh! We made Punicus into Tiphys the helmsman. In the *Argonautica* Tiphys dies on the journey back from Colchis.'

Flavia's eyes opened wide. 'Do you think he'll be the next to go?'

Nubia almost choked on her gum and they had to slap her on the back.

When she recovered she looked at them with her large amber eyes. 'And I am Hercules,' she whispered, 'who is being left behind by *Argo*.'

'Don't worry,' said Flavia, giving Nubia a reassuring hug. 'We would never abandon a good friend like you.'

*

The sun was low in the west when Nubia heard a sound that made her heart skip a beat: Tigris's alarm bark.

She stood with the plate of sea urchins poised above the polished table and slowly turned towards the stern platform, where Jonathan's big puppy stood barking.

'Great Neptune's beard!' Captain Geminus had turned from the tiller in annoyance. 'Someone stop that cacophony. Get that dog below!'

Nubia put the plate on the table and ran past the deckhouse and up the four steps to the stern platform. She arrived just before Flavia and Jonathan.

Tigris turned his head and whined up at them and Nubia almost fainted. Before her lay an empty expanse of glittering water. There was no skiff following the *Delphina*, not even a rope trailing behind.

Lupus had vanished.

SCROLL XI

'By all the gods! What was that boy thinking?'

Flavia could tell that her father was more upset than angry by the way he ran his hand through his hair.

'He wanted to find his mother,' said Jonathan.

'On the isle of Symi,' said Nubia.

'So he decided to row there?' cried Flavia's father.

Suddenly Flavia realised something.

'Pater!' she cried. 'The tow-rope.'

He turned and looked at her.

'It's gone!' she cried. 'If Lupus had untied his end it would be trailing behind in the water. But it's not here. That means Lupus didn't do it. Someone on board the *Delphina* did it!'

Lupus took a long drink from the water skin he had found in the *Cygnet* and looked around.

He had woken slightly before sunset to find himself adrift, surrounded by nothing but water and sky. His eyes were still swollen from weeping but he could see that the horizon was perfectly straight. There was no dark hump of an island and no white nick of a sail. He might have been alone in the world.

He knew he should be terrified but he felt strangely calm.

The *Delphina* had been sailing southeast, and on the previous nights the sun had set on over the right-hand steering oar. Lupus pushed out one of the oars in the skiff and turned it in the water until the skiff swung round to bring the lightest part of the sky onto her right side.

At least he could make sure he was travelling in the same direction as the *Delphina*, so that if she turned . . . And with this thought the fear began to seep in. Jove's wind had been favourable for the past four days. Since they had left Corinth it had been right behind them. And Lupus knew that no ship without oars could sail directly into the wind.

He needed help. He needed the gods. Lupus fingered the good luck charm around his neck and heard the little bronze bells tinkle.

'You don't need that,' said a quiet voice.

Lupus looked around, heart thumping. There was no one in the boat. No one in the water. No one but him for miles and miles.

The voice did not come again but the words still hung in his mind, not fading but growing stronger, heavier, more compelling.

You don't need that.

As Lupus stood up he realised his knees were trembling. He pulled the linen cord over his head and after only a moment's hesitation he threw the amulet into the sea. It broke the pearly skin of the water with barely a sound and then it was gone. But just as Lupus was about to sit down again he saw something. A moment earlier the horizon had been blank. But now he thought he could make out a smudge away to the northeast.

He wasn't sure whether it was land or just a cloud,

but he sat down in the skiff and took up the oars and began to row.

Twilight. The current was with him and the opalescent water was so smooth that it might have been oiled. The sky had deepened from mauve to lavender to violet, now pricked with stars. Glancing over his shoulder, Lupus caught sight of land silhouetted sharp and flat against a silvery glow on the dark horizon. And presently the glow became a lopsided moon which swam up among the stars like an enormous pearl bowl graciously tipping her light onto the sea, making a shining path straight towards the land.

Much later, he heard the sound of breakers and saw the white line of surf, and although the moon was now at her remotest place high above, she still smiled kindly. Lupus leapt out into the cold shock of black, chest-high water and felt the shifting slippery pebbles under his feet as he pulled the boat towards the beach. At last he fell exhausted onto the sand and slept.

The cheeping of tiny chaffinches woke Lupus just after dawn the next morning. Six of them were pecking in the coarse damp sand not two feet away. He watched them for a while but when he raised his head they flew off.

His mouth was dry and his hands were blistered, but apart from that he was unscathed. The previous night's magic seemed still to be with him, for he heard the chuckling of fresh water and soon he found a stream running down to the sea. Its water was pure and sweet. He brushed the sand from his cheek and he cupped his hands and he carefully drank.

Presently, Lupus wiped his mouth on the back of his arm and looked around. The crescent beach led up to a strand of grey-green tamarisk trees, with a few palm trees here and there. Beyond the trees rose a mountain, still violet-shadowed in the early morning.

All he had on him was his sea-green tunic and the leather belt which also served as a sling. He did not have sandals, for everyone went barefoot on board the ship. He did not even have his wax tablet and stylus because he had thrown them down in anger. Then he remembered what else he possessed. He went back to the skiff and untied the heavy rope that had attached the *Cygnet* to the *Delphina*. He coiled it and carefully put it out of sight under one of the benches. Then he found the empty water skin. He brought it to the stream and filled it as full as he could.

Lupus began to walk up towards the trees, his eyes scanning the mountainside for any sign of life. He did not know if he was on the mainland or on some island, but he felt there was something special about this place. The air was brilliantly pure, but there was a comforting weight to it, as if someone infinitely benevolent was watching over him. Was it his mother? He didn't think so. He remembered the voice in the boat – a man's voice – and the sense of peace that had filled him. This felt like that, only magnified one hundred times. His vision blurred, then cleared as he blinked away the tears filling his eyes.

Suddenly he stopped and sniffed. Wood smoke. And then another glorious smell, perhaps the most wonderful smell in the world. His stomach growled enthusiastically and although he was shipwrecked and destitute, Lupus felt like laughing.

The scent which filled his head was the smell of baking bread.

Lupus followed the scent of warm bread through the feathery tamarisk trees. Presently he stood before a small house built in the Roman style.

Outside the double doors were two plaster-covered pillars. Just as in Ostia or Rome, they were painted deep red to about the height of his shoulder. He stepped forward to knock at the front door, then hesitated and cautiously moved round the side of the house.

Standing on the other side of a circular courtyard with his back to Lupus was a dark-haired boy in a grey tunic. The boy was leaning to open the circular door of an outdoor oven. Plaster-covered and shaped like a beehive, the oven was raised on a platform so that it was almost as tall as the boy. Now the boy was inserting a large wooden paddle to scoop up half a dozen loaves of flat bread.

The courtyard was composed of black and white pebbles in a geometric design. As Lupus began to cross it, his bare foot crunched a leaf and the boy froze.

'Who's there?' The boy spoke in Greek, without turning around. And then in Latin: 'Domina?'

Lupus grunted no, and as the boy spun round the bread flew off the paddle and onto the pebbled floor.

'Oh Pollux!' the boy cursed, as half a dozen speckled hens appeared from among the trees and charged for the bread, clucking triumphantly.

Lupus lunged for the loaves and managed to reach all six before any of the hens. The soft discs were still hot, so he quickly dropped them on the plaster-covered ledge beside the oven door.

The boy turned his whole body towards Lupus, who smiled and gestured at the bread. But the boy did not look at Lupus or the bread or the hens. He stood with his head tipped to one side.

Then Lupus saw the milky film over his eyes and realised the boy was blind.

'Where are you?' asked the blind boy. 'Please don't taunt me.'

Lupus gently took the boy's hand and placed it on the disks of hot bread.

'Oh,' said the boy. 'Thank you. You startled me. Are you . . . ?' Here he moved his hand up Lupus's arm and touched his face and hair with quick, light fingers. 'You're not from the island, are you?' he said in Greek. 'What's your name? Mine is Pinchas.'

Lupus gently guided the boy's fingers to his mouth and then inside.

'Oh,' said the boy, his hand recoiling. 'I'm sorry. I can't see. And you can't speak. But . . . can you understand me?'

Lupus nodded, not minding that the boy was still lightly touching his head.

'Are you from this island?'

Lupus tipped his head back in the Greek 'no' and then remembered that Romans shook their heads for 'no'. So he shook his head.

'But you're Greek, aren't you?' The boy smiled. 'I can tell just by the way you moved your head. Are there other people here with you?'

Lupus shook his head.

'Were you shipwrecked?'

Lupus nodded and the boy gasped. Then: 'Are you hungry?'

Lupus grunted 'yes', and his nod was so violent that they both began to laugh. The boy groped for a loaf and tore it and handed a piece to Lupus.

And then – to Lupus's astonishment – he pronounced a blessing in Hebrew.

SCROLL XII

'Pinchas!' screeched a woman's voice. 'Pinchas, where are you? Where's that bread? If you're—'

The woman in the archway stared at Lupus and he stared back. She had frizzy red hair and pale skin and she wore a long unbelted tunic of cream linen.

'Who's this, Pinchas?' she said in Latin, not taking her eyes from Lupus.

'It's a boy, domina! And he's been shipwrecked. I hope you don't mind but I gave him some bread.'

'I do mind,' said the woman. Her tunic flapped about her as she strode across the pebbled courtyard to give Pinchas a cuff on the ear. 'Shipwrecked indeed!' She turned to Lupus.

Up close he could see that she was elderly, at least forty years old. She might have been pretty once, even beautiful, but her face wore a sour expression that looked as if it had been there for decades.

'Ask him where he's from,' she said to Pinchas in Latin.

'He can't speak, domina,' the boy replied in the same language. 'He has no tongue.'

'Wool fluff!' she snorted, but her eyes widened as Lupus shook his head, then opened his mouth and pointed in.

'Great Juno's girdle!' she exclaimed. 'You understand Latin!'

Lupus nodded.

'But you can't speak?' She peered into his mouth. 'Ah. I've seen that before. Criminal are you? Thief?'

Lupus shook his head angrily.

'Then what were you doing nosing around here?'

'He was shipwrecked, domina,' said Pinchas.

'Is that true?'

Lupus nodded.

She gave him a keen look. 'Are you from Rome?'

Lupus waggled his head – as if to say yes and no – then stepped over to the oven. He dipped his finger in some soot and wrote on the white plaster dome: OSTIA

'Great Juno's – You can read and write, too!' said the woman, raising her eyebrows. 'I don't suppose you have any news from Italia? Is Titus still emperor?'

Lupus grunted 'yes'.

Pinchas stepped forward. 'What's your name?' the blind boy asked him.

Lupus touched the soot again and wrote on the white plaster.

'Lupus?' said the woman with a snort. 'Not a very civilised name. Well, I'm Julia. Julia Aquila. You're the first visitor I've had in nearly half a year. I suppose I should invite you to breakfast. Pinchas! Take this bread and lead our guest into the triclinium. I'll go and see if I can find some fig cakes and the Calymnian honey.'

An hour later, Lupus's hand was aching and he had hardly eaten any of the food laid out on the table before him. Julia had found pen and ink and sheets of papyrus and she had forced him to answer all her questions in writing.

'That's enough,' said Julia at last.

Lupus reached for a piece of bread and honey almost as eagerly as she reached for the papyrus sheets. While she read and re-read what he had written, Lupus was able to wash down the bread and honey with warm goat's milk.

'So,' said Julia, at last. 'Berenice wore green emeralds with a green silk gown?'

Lupus nodded, chomping the bread with his molars, then throwing his head back to swallow.

'Wasn't it a bit . . . *overdone*?'

Lupus shook his head and gave a thumbs-up.

'So she's as beautiful as everyone says?'

Lupus nodded enthusiastically.

Julia heaved a deep sigh and put the sheets to one side. 'And now you're on your way to Rhodes to rescue some children who've been kidnapped?'

Lupus nodded.

'And you believe the people on board your ship will stop and come looking for you once they realise you're missing? Even though they have dozens of other children to save?'

Lupus hung his head, and nodded again.

'Well, I think they're fools to bother with you,' she said with a snort. 'But if you're convinced they'll return then I suggest you go up the mountain and make some sort of signal for them. This is a miserable, barren little rock but it has many bays and inlets. Even if they make their way here they may never find you. Take these sulphur sticks and make a fire of brush wood up on the bare part of the mountainside. Be sure to make a clearing first. This is only a hovel but I don't want it burnt to the ground. Pinchas will show you the path.'

It was very strange being led by a blind person, but Lupus allowed Pinchas to take his hand and guide him back across the pebbled courtyard, past the oven, through the feathery tamarisks to an inscribed boundary stone.

'Do you see the stone?' Pinchas asked Lupus.

Lupus grunted 'yes'.

'Do you see the path?'

Lupus grunted 'yes' again.

'It goes all the way up to the top of the mountain. But you shouldn't have to go all that way. Just go halfway, as far as the caves.'

Lupus squeezed Pinchas's hand to say thank you but the blind boy did not let go. 'Lupus,' he whispered. 'I heard my mistress talking about your mission. When I was seven, I was kidnapped from my home, near Antioch. They took me to a house in Rhodes. I served a man named Magnus. Have you heard of him?'

Lupus frowned.

'They also call him the Colossus of Rhodes.'

Lupus squeezed Pinchas's hand and grunted an excited 'yes'.

'In his house was a big dark smelly room. They took me there and put me with other children. And they forced us to make carpets. All day, every day. They told us that children are the best weavers. They kept the room dark, so the colours wouldn't fade. After a few years most of the children cough and some . . .' Pinchas stopped talking for a moment.

Lupus squeezed his trembling hand again.

'I'd only been there for three years when I began to lose my sight. At first I could still see the patterns, then only fuzzy blurs and colours. You try not to let them know, because if they find out—' he was weeping now and the tears flowed down his face '—if they find out you are blind, then they put you out and you have nowhere else to go. I was lucky because I spoke Latin, Greek and Aramaic. A man brought me here to help serve my mistress. But Lupus . . .' Now he was gripping Lupus's hand so hard that it hurt. 'Even the ones who go blind are the lucky ones. Not all the children they steal work in the carpet factory. Some of them . . . they take some of them away on a ship at the full moon, and nobody ever hears of them again.'

'Look!' cried Flavia, pointing. 'There on the mountainside. That's where the smoke is coming from.'

'Do you think it's a signal?' asked Jonathan.

'It must be. There's no other sign of life,' she said.

The *Delphina* was gliding into the crescent bay of a small island. Flavia's father had taken Punicus's advice and let the current carry the ship throughout the night.

'I see house behind trees,' said Nubia.

'I think I know where the smoke is coming from,' said Jonathan. 'There's a fire by those caves further up the mountainside.'

'I see him!' cried Nubia. 'I am seeing the Lupus!'

'By the gods you have good eyesight,' said a deep voice, and Flavia turned to see Flaccus close behind them. For once he wasn't chewing gum but Flavia could still smell the faint scent of mastic on his breath. She turned back to look at the thread of smoke ascending from the mountain.

'Where's Lupus, Nubia?' she said. 'I can't see him.'

'There!' cried Jonathan. 'I see him. He's by that cave. Waving his arms.'

'Oh! Yes! I see him!' squealed Flavia. She and Nubia put their hands on each other's shoulders and hopped up and down with joy.

'Where?' said Flaccus again, squinting at the island before them.

'See that little figure waving his arms?' laughed Flavia.

'No.'

'Do you see that cave in the mountain?' said Jonathan. 'Straight ahead?'

'I can't . . . not really. No.'

'Well then, do you see the smoke rising up into the sky?'

Flaccus squinted.

'You can't even see the smoke?' gasped Flavia.

'Which island is this?' asked Bato, joining them at the prow.

'I'm not sure,' said Flavia. 'Shall I ask pater?'

He nodded.

'PATER!!' bellowed Flavia in the direction of the helm. 'What's the name of this island?'

'We're just trying to find it,' he said, looking up from the chart spread out on the top of the deckhouse.

From the masthead above them Zosimus called down. 'I believe it's Patmos, sir. Nothing there but sponge-divers.'

Flavia saw Flaccus and Bato exchange a look.

'What?' she asked Bato. 'Have you heard of it?'

Bato nodded. 'Patmos is notorious. An island of political exile.'

'What?' said Nubia.

Flaccus explained: 'It's one of the places they send highborn Roman men and women who have committed terrible crimes.'

SCROLL XIII

'Do you think your friends will come ashore?' asked Julia Aquila, standing on the beach in the shadow of the tamarisks and watching the *Delphina* sail into the cove. 'My bath-house is small but Pinchas can heat the water in less than an hour.' She turned to look down at Lupus and he noticed she had powdered her face and stained her lips. She had also tied a belt around her thick waist. 'We could have a dinner party.'

Still breathing hard from his scramble down the mountainside, Lupus shrugged. He knew his friends would be in a hurry.

'You're probably right,' said Julia bitterly. 'They won't want to come. They never do. They're afraid my bad luck will wear off on them. I was exiled, you see. Exiled by Nero so he could seize my estate. Oh, how I detest this wretched island!' Julia turned and wove back through the trees towards the house. 'Pinchas!' she cried, pushing through the double doors. 'There you are, Pinchas! Say goodbye to Lupus. He's abandoning us.'

Lupus went into the small tablinum and took a wax tablet from the table.

THANK YOU FOR HELPING ME he wrote, and held it out to her.

'Yes,' she said gruffly. 'I'm too kind. That's my problem.'

Lupus pointed at Pinchas and then at himself.

'What about Pinchas?' She scowled.

CAN HE HELP ME PUSH OUT BOAT?

'Yes, I suppose so. He wants you to help him, Pinchas. Make sure you come straight back.'

'I'm sorry, Lupus,' said Pinchas a short time later. 'I think I understand why you're tugging my hand, but I can't come with you. I've seen what they do to run-away slaves.'

Pinchas was standing waist high in the sea, holding the edge of the bobbing skiff. 'Besides,' he said, 'My mistress needs me. She's not always as bad-tempered as she was today.'

Lupus leaned forward and gripped one of Pinchas's wet hands and grunted.

'Shalom, Lupus.' Pinchas gave the boat a push. 'I hope you come this way again some day. Or maybe I will meet you in Rome if my mistress is ever recalled.'

Lupus dipped his oars. Already he could hear Tigris's barks coming from the ship anchored behind him in the bay.

'Lupus, don't forget!' called Pinchas. 'The children always disappear from Rhodes on the night of the full moon. If you want to save them you only have five days left.'

A cheer greeted Lupus as soon as he stepped back onto the deck. He was hugged and ruffled and given butter-milk to drink and installed in Captain Geminus's leather captain's chair in the shade of the deckhouse awning.

But once the sail had filled and the *Delphina* was on a southeast course again, his friends grew quiet and presently he realised why. By going back for him, they had lost a day in their pursuit of the *Medea*.

'Don't worry, Lupus,' said Flavia, with forced brightness. 'We're almost sure to find the *Medea* in Rhodes.'

Lupus took out his wax tablet and wrote what he had learned from Pinchas: that Rhodes was indeed the base of a criminal called Magnus who forced some children to weave carpets and sent others away on the night of the full moon.

'The full moon is in five days,' said Flavia. 'Pater?' she called. 'Can we be in Rhodes in five days?'

'If this fair wind continues, we should be there the day after tomorrow,' he said from the tiller.

Later, when Flavia, Nubia, Jonathan and Zetes went down into the skiff with Atticus to fish for dinner, Lupus went to the prow. He had found a new retreat, a new place to think about his mother and his vow. If he climbed up the slanting foremast, he could sit on the small yard-arm with a foot dangling on either side. Now he rested there, hugging the mast and staring towards the place where Symi might appear on the dark blue horizon.

Footsteps creaked on the deck behind him and he turned his head to look.

It was only Zosimus. Zosimus and his pigeons.

Lupus unhooked his legs and slid down the polished foremast, then jumped lightly onto the deck. Zosimus grinned up at him. He was kneeling before his wicker cage. The door was open and he was reaching into it.

'Take Patroclus for a moment?' he asked.

Lupus nodded and extended his hands. As he took

the pigeon he remembered the vow and sacrifice he had made on the beach at Ostia. It had not been difficult to twist off the head of the pigeon.

Zosimus rose from the cage and gave Lupus a sharp look.

'You all right?' he asked.

Lupus nodded and held out the bird.

'Just hold him for another moment,' said Zosimus and began to roll the scrap of papyrus around the copper wire.

Lupus grunted and raised his eyebrows at the message.

Zosimus chuckled. 'Just a note to tell my old mother how we rescued you from the island. And also that we'll be in Cos tonight. Her family comes from there, though she grew up in Rhodes.' He paused for a moment, breathing heavily as he fixed the papyrus-wrapped wire around the pigeon's pink leg. Then, without looking up, he said, 'I hear your mother lives in Symi.'

Lupus stiffened but Zosimus kept his head down, still adjusting the message. 'You can't keep many secrets on board ship,' he said. 'I heard the Captain talking.' He glanced up at Lupus. 'Why don't you visit her? If my old mother were nearby, I'd want to pay her a call.'

Lupus shrugged, but his heart was beating hard. It was a good question. Why didn't he try to find her, now? They had five days until the full moon and they were only two days from Rhodes.'

'I'm sure Captain Geminus wouldn't mind,' continued Zosimus. 'He plans to spend the night in Cos and sail onto Rhodes the next morning. But with this breeze we could easily reach Symi tonight. And from

Symi it's only a few hours to Rhodes. There!' Zosimus stepped back. 'Of course, you and I can't tell the Captain what to do, but you could suggest it to his daughter. She might be able to convince him.'

Lupus gazed at Zosimus. If he could just find out whether his mother was still alive, he could help his friends rescue the kidnapped children with an easy mind. Then he could sail back to Symi and sell the *Delphina* and with the money he and his mother could live happily for many years.

In his hands the pigeon stirred and he realised he was holding it too tightly.

'Go on,' said Zosimus gently. 'Let the pigeon go. Let him fly home to mother.'

'But Lupus,' whispered Flavia a short time later. 'We can't stop at Symi now. We have to find the captured children. We've already lost our best chance to catch the *Medea*.'

I ONLY WANT TO SPEND ONE NIGHT Lupus wrote on his tablet. TO SEE IF SHE'S STILL THERE

He and his friends and Captain Geminus were in the deckhouse studying the map laid out on the table there.

'I did consider spending the night at Symi, Lupus,' said Captain Geminus, 'but according to Punicus, that could pose a few problems. It's close to the mainland, and mischievous breezes play havoc with navigation.'

He lowered his voice even more. 'I know you're desperate to see your mother, but can't you wait until after we've been to Rhodes? Once we've rescued the children, we can drop you off on Symi and you can spend as much time as you like with your mother. The rest of your life, if you want!'

Lupus looked around at his friends. Jonathan had his head down, examining Tigris's fur for ticks, but Flavia and Nubia looked back at him with solemn eyes. Lupus lowered his gaze and pretended to stare at the chart. He didn't want to see the mixture of reproach and sympathy in the girls' faces. His heart was pounding hard and he remembered the vow he had made on Ostia's beach.

Finally he took a deep breath and tapped the island of Symi on the chart.

'Very well,' said Flavia's father. 'You're the ship's owner. Symi it is. I'll give the order to alter our course immediately. We can pick up a cargo of sponges while we're there. Don't look so glum!' he added, giving Lupus a pat on the shoulder. 'You might see your mother tonight.'

Symi was gold and green in the setting sun, and now that the island lay before him, Lupus remembered it well. His eyes hungrily took in the familiar caves and grottoes dotting the seaside cliffs. A flock of sheep followed their own lengthening shadows up the scrubby mountainside and he could hear the faint, haunting sound of their bells clanking. But what brought the memories rushing back most strongly was a whiff of the scent of Symi: a mixture of thyme, dillweed and rosemary. He closed his eyes and inhaled and the thought occurred to him that even if he were blind like Pinchas he would know his home by this smell.

He kept his eyes closed and tried to see his mother's face.

Nothing. Just the honey-coloured hair.

Lupus opened his eyes again and blinked away the

tears. Maybe when he saw her he would remember her, as he now remembered Symi.

Presently they rounded the headland. The sun and wind were abruptly blotted out by the island, and the ship began to lose momentum. But there was just enough breeze to bring them slowly around another point and Lupus finally saw the crescent beach and the tiny house – like a cube of white cheese – that had been his home.

'Is that your house?' Nubia's voice was soft beside him.

Lupus nodded without taking his eyes from it. His mother would be there. He was sure of it. And he knew he would recognise her as soon as she opened the door. Then he would have a family again.

A faint breeze caressed the mainsail, making the painted dolphin shiver in the grey light of dusk. Captain Geminus gave an order and the artemon at the front unfurled, but their progress was still barely perceptible. Lupus's cove was too shallow for the *Delphina*, so they had to carry on around one more promontory to reach the main harbour, a sheltered tongue of water with hills rising up steeply around it. Now the wind had died completely, so Captain Geminus ordered the skiff round to the front. Presently the *Cygnet*'s oars rose and fell as she towed the *Delphina* towards a vacant berth.

By now it was almost dark, but Lupus could make out the shapes of men gathering on the dock, silhouetted by the torches of a tavern behind them. His heart had been thumping for nearly an hour, and now it beat so hard he almost felt sick.

The *Delphina* finally nudged up against the quayside

on their right, and Lupus turned his gaze north, towards the dark shipyard and little promontory which they had just rounded.

Greek voices calling up: laughter, questions, welcome, the arrival of the harbourmaster, roused from his bed but cheerful, and finally the thud of the heavy wooden gangplank. Tigris was the first one down it, his tail wagging and his nose low, questing for new smells. Lupus followed him with trembling knees and blurred vision. At the bottom he nearly put a foot wrong and fell between the ship and the land, but calloused hands caught him and laughing men set him firmly on solid ground.

He was home.

Tigris led the torchlit procession almost as if he knew where Lupus was going. He led them around the dark promontory, along the curve of a shallow bay, and past the silent shipyard. As they went along the dirt path, more and more people joined them, some coming down the steep whitewashed steps on their left, some coming from behind. They carried torches, and in the flickering light Nubia saw that many of the islanders had thick, coarse honey-gold hair. She remembered that Lupus's mother was called Melissa, which meant honey in Greek.

She also saw the glinting eyes of feral cats lurking in the shadows. One or two mewed, then caught Tigris's scent and disappeared into the night. Nubia could hear the mutterings of the people around her, but she could only catch one or two words of their island Greek: the names 'Lukos', 'Melissa' and 'poor boy'.

Lupus must have heard their whispers, too, but he

ignored them and as Nubia watched him hurrying forward with his torch, her heart melted for him. His slender neck made him look so vulnerable from behind.

At last the path carried them round the base of a jutting cliff and brought them to the lone house at the foot of the hillside. It faced a small beach and the black sea beyond.

Lupus hesitated and stopped but some of the villagers were calling. 'Aphrodite, he's home! Your great-grandson is home!' And Nubia saw the crowd push him forward.

A light moving in a square window of the ghostly white house, then another, and then – just as Lupus was about to knock – a door opened, revealing a tiny, ancient woman with wrinkled skin and a wart on her forehead. She wore a black shift and her dishevelled hair was a white cloud around her head.

'What is it?' she cried, her eyes gleaming in the flickering light of a dozen torches. Then she saw Lupus standing there, holding his torch up and looking into the house. 'Lukos?' she cried. 'Lukos?'

Nubia took Lupus's flaming torch a moment before the old woman threw her arms around him. She was wailing and babbling, and at first Nubia could not understand her words. They came too fast and they were mixed with too many tears.

But presently one phrase chimed in Nubia's understanding. One phrase in Greek that the old woman kept repeating. 'Too late.' She was saying to Lupus. 'You're too late.'

SCROLL XIV

Lupus's great-grandmother released him from her embrace but now all the other islanders were pressing forward to touch him. 'Son of the murdered man. Melissa's little boy. Lukos.' They were talking at him and around him, kissing him, peering into his mouth, hugging him, pinching his cheeks.

He snarled as he felt a sudden panic.

'Great Neptune's beard!' bellowed Flavia's father in his deck voice. Although he spoke in Latin, the Greeks shrank back at the sight of the tall fair-haired Roman moving forward and brandishing his torch.

At the same moment Lupus saw an old man pushing his way through the crowd from another direction. He was shouting 'Enough! Enough!' in Greek.

The old man glared round at the villagers, his leathery face creased with disapproval. 'Can you not see the boy is exhausted? Let him catch a breath. Go back to your beds. What kind of hospitality is this, that we do not even allow a son of Symi to rest after his voyage? Go! GO! Off with you! You will see him tomorrow.'

The islanders reluctantly began to disperse, still chattering and darting curious looks back at Lupus even as they disappeared into the night.

When they had all gone, the leathery man pulled a wooden chair up to the battered wooden table under the arbour. He gestured for Captain Geminus and the children to sit.

'Aphrodite!' he said to the old woman. 'Bring us wine. And food.'

Lupus's great-grandmother hobbled off and returned a moment later with a tray of cups and jugs. As the man began to mix wine with the water, she disappeared back into the house. When he had passed each of them a cup, he raised his own, then tipped it. A thin stream of liquid spattered onto the ground.

'A libation to Poseidon,' he said, 'and to Apollo, in thanks for bringing Melissa's son back to us.' Lupus followed his example and the others poured out libations, too.

Aphrodite returned a moment later with flat bread and olives and a bowl full of tiny pink shrimp. When they had all eaten and their cups had been refilled, the leather-faced man leaned back and nodded at Lupus.

'My name is Andreas,' he said, still speaking Greek. 'I am one of the elders of this village. Before you sleep, Lukos, you must know the events of the last week.'

Aphrodite started to say something in her quavering voice but Andreas silenced her with a patting motion of his hand.

'Two weeks ago,' he said. 'The first ship of the season came from Rome, to trade with us for sponges. There was a man on board from Ostia, and he told us your story, Lukos. He told us that you were alive and that you had finally taken revenge on the one who murdered your father.' Andreas turned his head and spat on the ground before continuing. 'When your mother Melissa heard this, she was beside herself with joy. But then she grew very quiet. When we asked what the matter was, she told us that three years ago she had made a vow to Apollo.'

Andreas reached for the jug and poured himself another cup of wine, then drank it down neat.

In that brief moment of silence, Lupus heard the torches crackling. He heard Flavia asking her father in a whisper what the old man was saying. He heard his great-grandmother weeping quietly. He could even hear the faint sound of little waves sighing onto the beach.

'Your mother thought you were in Italia,' said Andreas quietly. 'If she had known you were on your way here . . .'

Lupus lifted his shoulders and stuck out his chin to ask: What?

'Your mother Melissa left Symi three days ago.'

Lupus felt as if he had been kicked in the stomach.

'Melissa left Symi?' repeated Flavia in Greek, and then said in Latin, 'Where did she go?'

'Where did she go?' asked Captain Geminus in Greek.

'She left on a ship bound for Rhodes,' said Andreas, 'but nobody knows where she might have gone from there. All we know is that it must have been a very solemn vow she took. She left all her belongings behind, and she told us she would never see us again.'

Early the next morning, Lupus slammed his wax tablet down on the table before Captain Geminus. WHY AREN'T WE GOING TO RHODES?

Flavia's father slowly looked up from his chart. 'Lupus,' he said in a low voice, 'it was your decision to come to Symi. We can't go anywhere for the moment. There's not a breath of wind. Even if they tow us out of the harbour, the current would only carry us onto the rocks. I warned you about this.'

Lupus picked up his wax tablet and briefly thought about hurling it down. Then he remembered how his stylus had wounded Nubia, and he managed to resist the impulse. He let his arm drop.

'Lupus.' Captain Geminus stood and opened a small bronze box on the table. 'Here. Take these coins. Go and make an offering at the sanctuary up there on the hill. Take Flavia and the others if you like. Ask the gods to send us *Skiron* or *Zephyrus*, or some other favourable breeze. Then spend an hour or two with your great-grandmother. Pay your respects at your father's grave. Come back at noon. If Andreas and the other elders are correct, and if the gods answer your prayer, the breeze might have risen by then.'

Lupus felt the captain's hand on his shoulder. 'Go on Lupus. Once we leave, who knows when we'll come this way again?'

In the end, Lupus went alone. He found his family tomb on the slope above the little house, and the tears came again as he read the inscription below his father's urn. He had not thought to bring an offering so he went back out into the bright sunshine and gathered a handful of wild flowers: red poppies, white daisies, purple trumpets, and wild roses.

Then he visited his great-grandmother. But she was old and tearful and illiterate. She could not read what he wrote, and she kept clutching at him with her claw-like hands.

Finally he squirmed free of her embrace and went to stand on the beach, at the spot where he and his father had pulled up the boat that fateful morning. He looked out over the water and in his mind he said 'Farewell.'

Half an hour later he walked up the gangplank of his ship, and as he stepped carefully down with his right foot he felt a cool breeze touch his cheek.

The *Delphina* was ready to sail.

But it was not the wind they wanted. As soon as they left the protection of Symi's harbour, a short, choppy sea began to batter the *Delphina*. The dolphin on the sail shuddered and writhed and the ship moved forward with an uneasy twisting motion.

Lupus climbed the rope ladder up to the masthead, but the *Delphina* was yawing so wildly that at times there was nothing between him and the cobalt-blue sea far below.

The wind buffeted them past more landmarks re-membered from his childhood. The tawny strip of mainland which his father had called Lizard's Tail passed on his left and straight ahead he saw Poseidon's Road. This latter was a strange, perfectly straight line of dark water and breaking surf in the middle of the sea. It caused no harm to ships but nevertheless the sailors all made the sign against evil when they left it behind.

As he gazed down to the deck below, he could see Flavia and Jonathan at the port rail. Nubia stood in the V of the prow, helping Zosimus send a message. She laughed as the ship reared like a horse and she almost lost hold of the pigeon. But a moment later he heard the flutter of wings and Zosimus's usual cry of 'Go with Hermes!'

As he watched the pigeon fly up and up into the sky, then wheel to the southeast, Lupus wished he could fly to his mother.

But even if he had wings like a bird he would not have known where to find her.

Flavia and Jonathan had moved back to the stern platform, and Lupus saw Nubia beckon him down before she joined them. Now their three heads were bent over something.

Lupus let himself carefully down the rope ladder, then staggered over the bucking deck to the stern.

'Is it in code?' Jonathan was asking, as Flavia unrolled a tiny scrap of papyrus.

'I don't think so.' She reached out to clutch the rail as the ship lurched. 'The writing's just very small and it's in Greek. It talks about Symi and Rhodes. I think that word means "moon". Oh, there you are, Lupus! Can you read this?'

Lupus took the papyrus. The wave of nausea that rose up in his throat was not caused by the ship's twisting motion, but by the message he held in his hand.

'What?' hissed Flavia. 'What does it say?'

Lupus took out his wax tablet and began to write. He noticed his hand was shaking as he translated the message taken from the pigeon's leg:

LEFT SYMI MIDDAY. I WILL TRY TO DELAY THEM BUT IT WILL BE DIFFICULT WITHOUT

AROUSING MORE SUSPICION. BEWARE. WE COULD BE IN RHODES BEFORE THE FULL MOON. I WILL KEEP YOU INFORMED. Z.

SCROLL XV

'Zosimus is the traitor!' said Bato as he read the message on the scrap of papyrus. He winced as he sat forward on one of the bags of salt in the dim hold. 'He must be spying for Magnus. You're sure he didn't see you take this?'

'I am most sure he did not see me,' said Nubia.

'What aroused your suspicions?'

Flavia replied. 'Zosimus sent a pigeon this morning, while we were still in port. Why send another this afternoon? Also, they always head in the opposite direction from Ostia. They've been flying to Rhodes, haven't they?'

'Probably,' said Bato.

'Furthermore,' said Flavia, 'Zosimus is one of the most experienced sailors on board. He could easily have loosened the halyard and untied the skiff's rope. Earlier in the voyage he probably oiled other ropes to make them slip out of Silvanus's hands. I think that's what Silvanus was going to tell me before he disappeared. Also, Zosimus can read and write. If I hadn't been so suspicious of Floppy, I would have realised that Zosimus was the culprit a long time ago.'

'And he was in a position to make sure Silvanus didn't return to the ship,' said Bato grimly. 'I should have seen it, too! We must seize him quickly. If

Zosimus suspects that we're onto him and alerts Magnus in Rhodes we'll never crack this ring.'

The *Delphina* lurched and Bato winced as he fell sideways against a bag of salt. 'I can't do much, I'm afraid,' he said. 'I think my collar-bone is cracked.'

'Don't worry,' said Flavia. 'Pater is strong.'

'We'll need someone else to help your father,' said Bato. 'Cornered men can be surprisingly vicious.'

'Flaccus is strong,' said Jonathan.

'I don't like him and I still don't trust him,' said Flavia. 'Look at that nasty black eye he gave you.'

'That wasn't his fault,' said Jonathan. 'I let my guard down when we were boxing.'

'I think it's time you trusted Valerius Flaccus,' said Bato to Flavia, and he stretched his good hand towards Jonathan. 'Please,' he said, 'help me up.'

'Wait!' cried Flavia. 'We should send another message. Something that will make Magnus – or whoever it is – think there's no problem. That other pigeon flew off without its message.'

'Good idea,' said Bato. 'But it's my writing arm that's been hurt. I don't know if I can imitate this handwriting, especially as it's written so small.'

'Lupus can do it, can't you, Lupus?'

Lupus nodded, his eyes bright for the first time since they'd left Symi.

They bent their heads over his wax tablet and presently they composed a response in Latin. Flavia went to find pen, ink, and papyrus while Bato and Lupus translated the message into Greek. Then Lupus carefully copied the Greek translation onto a scrap of papyrus the same size as the stolen one.

'Perfect!' said Bato. 'Here, Nubia. Wrap this around the copper wire.'

While Nubia was doing this, Flavia picked up Lupus's wax tablet and re-read their new message:

UNDERGOING MAJOR REPAIRS HERE IN SYMI. WE WILL BE AT LEAST A WEEK. I WILL KEEP YOU INFORMED. Z.

Nubia moved carefully towards the prow. In this strange choppy sea, the deck was not always where her foot expected it to be. Far above her, a feathery glaze of clouds had turned the sun to copper and made the sea the colour of lead. The sound of the wind in the rigging was a note higher than it had been when she went below. And she felt the familiar pressure on the top of her head that told her a storm was coming.

She picked her way among the ropes and anchor to the prow and knelt before the pigeon cage. Down here at the front of the *Delphina* it was sheltered, and she felt the sun's faint warmth on her back. Folding back the cloth that covered the cage, Nubia opened the wicker door. The pigeons cooed and puffed at her, their red eyes blinking. She almost chose Agamemnon, the biggest, but Odysseus was her favourite, so she took him instead. She held him close to her chest the way Zosimus had taught her, and closed the door again. Then she stood up and started to fix the papyrus-wrapped wire around his foot, staggering a little as the ship rocked.

She was dreading the moment when Zosimus would notice her, and presently he did.

'What are you doing, Nubia?' she heard him call

down from the masthead. 'Sending a message to my old mum?'

Nubia kept her head bent over the pigeon, pretending not to hear him. Her hands trembled as she hurried to attach the papyrus-wrapped wire to the pigeon's leg.

'Nubia? Nubia!' she heard his voice moving down from the sky behind her, felt the faint vibration as he jumped down onto the deck. She did not hear his bare feet above the sound of the wind and the crack of canvas, but she did hear a startled grunt just as she finished securing the message to Odysseus's foot. She tossed the pigeon into the air and watched it fly towards Rhodes. Then she turned to see Captain Geminus tying Zosimus's hands behind his back.

'What are you doing, sir?' asked the little sailor with a nervous laugh.

'Maybe this will help you understand,' said Bato, limping forward and holding up the original message in his left hand. He winced as the *Delphina* bucked and it was obvious to Nubia that his injured arm still hurt. It must have been obvious to Zosimus as well, because quick as lightning he writhed free of the captain's grip and charged Bato with his head down.

Nubia gasped as Bato collapsed onto the rolling deck, retching and gasping. Flavia screamed and Tigris began to bark.

But Flaccus had seized the little Rhodian in a powerful grip and now Captain Geminus was beside him, breathing hard, and here was Atticus in his leather apron with a bloody cleaver in his hand.

All three were tall, strong men but even so, they had difficulty subduing Zosimus. Presently their captive stopped struggling and stared panting round at them with the same wild look Nubia had once seen in the eyes of a cornered jackal.

Flavia's father must have seen it, too, for he shouted to Lupus to bring a strong cord. Lupus ran to get a length of rope while Flavia and Nubia helped Bato to his feet.

As the three men pulled Zosimus to the mast, he started thrashing again and uttered a stream of oaths that made Nubia's face grow hot. Only when they had lashed him to the mainmast with thick cord did he stop shouting.

Nubia felt the tears fill her eyes. She had liked him and trusted him.

'Tell us what you know,' said Bato, his face pale and his good hand pressed to his stomach. 'Tell us who your patron is and what you're planning.'

Zosimus spat at him. 'I won't tell you anything.'

'We'll see about that,' said Flaccus, stepping forward and drawing back his fist.

'Stop!' cried Flavia's father, and when Flaccus looked at him for an explanation, he said: 'Not in front of the girls.'

Flaccus nodded at Captain Geminus and glared at Zosimus. 'You're lucky he stopped me,' he growled, clenching his fists to make his muscles look bigger.

In the struggle Zosimus's striped felt cap had been pulled down over one eyebrow. He reminded Nubia of a funny acrobat she had once seen in Ostia's forum. That – and the release of tension – gave her a sudden urge to giggle. As she caught Flavia's eye she knew her friend was thinking the same thing. It was like a scene from a comic play: the outraged young hero about to pound the wily slave.

The two girls hugged, and each buried a giggling face in the other's shoulder. When Nubia heard Bato say, 'You Rhodian dog! You've made those little girls cry!' her shoulders shook even more.

But she stopped laughing when she heard Zosimus cry, 'No! Not my pigeons! Don't hurt my birdies!'

Lupus ignored Flavia's scream and twisted the pigeon's head from its body. Then he tossed the twitching, bubbling bird at its owner's feet.

'No!' cried Zosimus, and as Lupus reached into the cage and grimly removed another bird: 'I'll tell you! Magnus! I work for Magnus.'

'And he lives on Rhodes?' Bato's face had regained some of its colour and now he stepped forward.

'Yes,' said Zosimus. 'Rhodes Town. Below the sanctuary of Helios. He . . . His house is on the Street of the Coppersmiths. He has a factory there, a carpet factory.'

'And that's where he takes the children?'

Zosimus hung his head. 'Yes. Most of them. They have sharp eyesight, clever fingers.' He looked up at them. 'They're well-treated. They're fed and clothed and they sleep all together in a nice big room. They make beautiful carpets. And after a few years we let them go.'

'Then why do none of them ever return?' asked Bato.

'Most of them? What do you mean "most of them"?' said Flaccus at the same time.

Zosimus looked from one to the other.

'What did you mean when you said "most of them"?'

repeated Flaccus, stepping forward and clenching his fists again.

'I . . . We . . . Magnus sends some of them on to Asia. To a buyer in Caria,' said Zosimus. 'I don't know his name.'

'Which ones?' said Flavia's father.

Zosimus stared down at the deck as it rose and tilted and sank beneath them.

Lupus held out a pigeon and slowly started to twist its head.

'The pretty ones!' screamed Zosimus.

Lupus eased his grip on the pigeon's neck and stared.

'We send the pretty ones to Asia.' Zosimus dropped his voice so that it was barely audible above the sound of the wind in the rigging. 'Pretty girls and pretty boys, that's who we send.'

'You vile dog,' growled Flaccus.

'Hypocrite!' Zosimus lifted his angry face towards Flaccus. 'You think you're better than the rest of us, but you're not.' He spat on the deck. 'Where do you think your pretty slave-boy came from?'

Flaccus froze, and in the brief silence Lupus heard the wind moan in the rigging.

'What do you mean?' Flaccus glanced at Zetes, who stood quietly against the rail watching them. The wind whipped his silky golden hair across his beautiful face. 'What do you mean by that?' repeated Flaccus.

'He's one of ours,' laughed Zosimus. 'Nine or ten years ago. I'd never forget that one. He was about four or five. Beautiful even then. Where did they tell you he was from? Gaul? Britannia?'

'Germania,' Flaccus's voice was trembling. 'He was a

gift on my ninth birthday. My father told me he was from Germania.'

Zosimus laughed. 'That boy's no German. As I remember, his father is prefect of the fleet at Ravenna.'

Flaccus's tanned face grew pale and he clutched the table to steady himself.

Zosimus spat again. 'That's right. He's as highborn as you are. And if his father ever found out you've been enjoying him as your slave he'd have your head on a platter.'

SCROLL XVI

The wind groaned in the rigging and snapped at the sails. It whipped at Flavia's tunic and made her skin break out in gooseflesh. Beneath her feet, the deck still moved with its strange twisting motion. Tied to the mast, Zosimus was crying, the tears running down his narrow cheeks. But she was only vaguely aware of these things.

She was watching Flaccus.

They all were. He was on his knees, head down, bloody hands tugging his hair, the feathered corpses of half a dozen headless pigeons scattered around him.

Flavia did not move. None of them did. Even Tigris was still.

Presently the beautiful boy Zetes knelt beside Flaccus and patted his young master's shaking back. He was weeping, too.

It may have been the writhing deck, but Flavia suddenly felt that nothing in her life was solid anymore.

While Atticus gathered up the feathered corpses, Lupus went down to the hold to watch the other men tie Zosimus to one of the iron rings.

Presently Lupus came back up on deck. Although only a short time had passed, the sky was now the colour of dirty wool and a gust of wind almost knocked him off his feet.

Flavia's father was back at the helm, bellowing orders to his two remaining crew members. Bare feet planted on deck, bald Punicus and grey-haired Atticus were trying to pull the ropes called brails that would raise the heavy mainsail, but they were struggling.

'Lupus!' Captain Geminus called out. 'Can you take the helm for a moment?'

Lupus nodded and staggered across the plunging deck to grasp the polished tiller. He was amazed at the strength it required to hold it steady and he gritted his teeth as Captain Geminus joined his crew at the ropes. Slowly the painted dolphin disappeared as the sail gathered itself up towards the yard-arm. Finally, the *Delphina*'s crew secured the brails to the polished pins and Lupus breathed a sigh of relief as Punicus took over the helm.

At that precise moment Lupus heard Captain Geminus bellow, 'Hang on tight! Everyone, hang on!'

Lupus turned to see an enormous wave rushing towards them like a grey-green mountain of glass. Uttering a Phoenician oath, Punicus pushed the tiller hard, bringing the *Delphina*'s nose around to take the wave head on. Lupus barely had time to grip the stern rail before his ship thrust her prow almost straight up to the sky, then plunged forward with a sickening drop as the great wave slid smoothly under her keel.

'The wind has changed!' cried Captain Geminus. 'It's the *Africus*!' He made the sign against evil along with the other members of his crew. 'The water's too deep to drop anchor. But we've got to find shelter. We'll have to run before the wind with just the artemon. And we'll have to haul the skiff on board and make her fast. Lupus, I'm two crew members down. Will you stay on deck?'

Lupus nodded and breathed a sigh of relief when he saw that Jonathan and Zetes had come to help him.

They had barely closed the hatch when the *Delphina* gave such a violent lurch that Flavia and Nubia were thrown across the width of the ship. Their heads cracked together hard. Tied to his ring at the other end of the dim hold, Zosimus laughed through his cloth gag.

'Wedge yourselves between bags of salt,' gasped Bato. 'But help me first.'

Flaccus moved out of the shadows to help Flavia wedge Bato, then he helped the girls.

'Thank you,' said Flavia, rubbing the sore spot on her head.

Flaccus nodded bleakly, then sat on a bag of salt beside Bato with his head in his hands. 'Germania. My father told me he was from Germania,' he said presently. 'I was only nine years old. How was I to know the boy was freeborn?'

Bato shook his head wearily. 'Don't worry, Valerius. These things happen. That's why we're trying to crack this ring.'

'But it's terrible,' repeated Flaccus. 'By the gods, I don't even know his real name. I should have guessed he was highborn. He has all the qualities: bearing, beauty, nobility . . .'

'And he's brave,' said Flavia coldly. 'He's up on deck now, helping pater and Jonathan and Lupus.'

Flaccus lifted his face from his hands and looked at her. His expression was no longer aloof, but vulnerable.

'You're right,' he said after a moment. 'Zetes is braver than I am. Here I am, weeping like a child . . .' He brushed his hair from his eyes and rose unsteadily to his feet. 'I'm going up.' He glanced over at Zosimus, uttering muffled threats and struggling against his bonds at the far end of the hold. 'Are you going to be all right down here? With him making that noise?'

The three of them nodded.

Flaccus started towards the hatch, then turned aside and took a few lurching steps to his hammock. He removed something from a leather satchel nearby, then staggered back and squatted beside Flavia. Her eyes widened as he took her hand and pressed something cool and round and waxy and fragrant into it.

'Take this lemon, Flavia,' he said, 'I have a feeling we're in for a rough time.'

It wasn't until after he had gone that Flavia realised it was the first time he had called her by name.

Lupus sat high on the mainmast.

The ill-omened south wind was driving them back the way they had come, undoing all their hard-won progress. Now it tore at the crests of the waves and shrieked in the rigging like some malevolent harpy.

Lupus's legs were hooked over the yard-arm and he hugged the mast. Behind him, wedging him in, was the very top of the rope ladder. From this safe vantage point he could see any approaching rocks and he shouted down warnings with his tongueless mouth and pointed towards the danger.

In this way they managed to skirt the southernmost shore of Symi and other rocks and islands that could not be identified in this howling world of sea and spray.

Nubia shivered in the hold of the ex-slave-ship *Vespa*.

She did not know how long the storm lasted or what Flavia's father and the others were doing on deck. All she knew was that the *Delphina* was being driven in some new direction. They were wedged between their bags of salt, but Nubia could hear the amphoras grinding against each other and the timbers of the ship groaning.

Despite sniffing the lemon which Flavia had pierced with her fingernails Nubia still felt cold and nauseous. Worse, she felt a deep despair. Was it her destiny to die in the hold of this ship?

She searched the timbers above her for the image of the woman. Finally she found it. 'Oh mother!' she whispered in her own language. 'Please help us. Please save us from the storm.'

With dusk came the portent.

The world was deep purple when one terrible thunderclap filled the whole sky, loud enough to split the cosmos. Lupus clung to the trembling mast and felt the air around him crackle with terror.

Presently he saw the dark boiling clouds move off to the northwest, towards the part of the sky that was palest. The stinging rain softened a little, and Lupus thought the worst of it was over. But now the men on deck were crying out in horror. Lupus squinted into the twilight, trying to see what new terror they had spotted, which rocks or reef he had missed. But they were not looking ahead. They were pointing straight up at him. Punicus was kneeling on the deck and at the helm Captain Geminus had a look of amazement on his face.

'Castor and Pollux!' cried Atticus, and despite his age he began to dance like a child on the wildly gyrating deck. 'We're saved!'

Lupus wondered if the whole crew had gone mad. Then he saw something that made him nearly leap off the mast into the black water below. On the very end of the yard-arm, the spar on which he perched, blazed a blue star.

Atticus was still dancing and pointing and Lupus followed his finger to see a similar star on the other end of the yard, only a few feet away from him. Then, to his utter amazement, the blue stars became flames: giant twin flames burning at either end of the *Delphina*'s yard-arm. They burned, but they did not consume.

SCROLL XVII

Nubia felt the ship run easier now. It was still pitching and bucking, but there was a steady rhythm now, less frantic. Outside, the roar of the wind had softened and she knew they were through the worst of the storm. And with that knowledge she finally sank into deep, dreamless sleep.

It seemed only a few moments later that she was aware of Flavia gently shaking her awake and extending a copper beaker of water.

Nubia washed the sour taste from her mouth and blinked as the pure light of morning poured down through the open hatch. She was stiff from lying wedged between bags of salt, but she managed to follow Flavia up onto the brilliant sunlit deck. A glance showed the *Delphina* battered but whole, and now gliding into a beautiful cove. On her right was a city of coloured marble – the most beautiful city she had ever seen – rising in tiers like the seats in an amphitheatre. She saw porticoes, colonnades, temples, fountains and even a theatre.

'Pater says it's Cnidos,' whispered Flavia in her ear. 'Come on. We're going to give thanks for surviving the storm.' Flavia took her hand and led her up to the stern platform where the others waited beside the little altar.

Then Nubia gasped. The wooden swan's head had been torn away by the storm. Only a ragged stump remained.

'It doesn't matter.' Captain Geminus was pale and unshaven, but his eyes shone. 'Last night,' he said, 'the gods showed their mercy. When the storm was at its worst, Castor and Pollux came and sat on either side of the yard-arm.'

'Oh!' cried Flavia. 'The sea stars that Admiral Pliny wrote about?'

Captain Geminus nodded. 'And something else that I have heard of but never seen.'

Nubia and the others all looked at him. Even Tigris was quiet.

'Before the twins settled on the yard-arm they shone round Lupus's head. Like a garland of blue light.'

Nubia stared at Lupus. He seemed as surprised as they did.

'It was a portent, Lupus,' said Punicus in his light voice. 'Your whole head shone. The gods have chosen you for some great task.' There was such reverence in his voice that for a moment Nubia thought the big Phoenician might fall at Lupus's feet and worship him.

Flavia's father solemnly covered his head with a fold of his toga and turned to the battered altar.

'Castor and Pollux,' he said presently, 'we thank you for coming to our aid and for saving us from the storm. Venus, we thank you for bringing us safely to your beautiful harbour of Cnidos. Please accept this offering until the proper one can be made.' He carefully laid a tiny bronze model of a sheep on the altar.

'And now that we have given thanks,' he said, pulling the toga from his head. 'Let's have something to eat before we begin the repairs. I believe that wonderful aroma is Atticus's pigeon stew.'

'No news of the *Medea* or any other slave-traders, I'm afraid,' said Captain Geminus, coming up the gangplank with a smiling young man close behind him. 'But Alexandros here and some of his friends have offered to help us repair the *Delphina*.'

'What does he say about all the jellyfish?' asked Flavia from the rail. 'I've never seen so many before.' She looked down at the hundreds of grey blobs floating in the harbour water.

Her father said something to the young man, who turned to Flavia and replied in broken Latin.

'These ones are dead,' said Alexandros. 'The storm kills them.'

'Can they still sting?' asked Nubia.

'Oh yes,' he said with a gap-toothed grin. 'They sting very good.'

Flavia shuddered, then turned as the sound of Greek curses rose up from the hatchway. Bato and Flaccus were hauling Zosimus out onto the deck. His hands were still tied behind him, but they had removed his gag.

'I'm leaving you here, in prison,' said Bato to Zosimus. 'Later, I'll take you back to Rome to stand trial. But first I want a few more answers.'

'You killed all my pigeons!' His red-rimmed eyes blazed. 'Why should I tell you anything?'

'Because if you don't,' said Flaccus, as they dragged him to the rail, 'we're going to toss you in for a swim.'

When Zosimus saw the undulating carpet of jellyfish his eyes grew wide.

'Now,' said Bato, 'tell us where they take the children on the full moon.'

Zosimus hesitated.

'Tell us!' shouted Flaccus, physically lifting the little man over the rail.

'Halicarnassus!' cried Zosimus. 'They take them to Halicarnassus.'

'Who's in Halicarnassus?' asked Flaccus. 'Who takes the children?'

'I don't know!'

Flaccus lifted Zosimus a fraction higher.

'Nobody knows, only Magnus!'

'What about Silvanus,' asked Flavia. 'What did you do with him? Did you kill him?'

'No. I just tied him up and left him in a cistern. I swear on my mother's eyes that I'm telling the truth.'

Flaccus eased Zosimus back down onto the deck.

'Speaking of your mother,' said Captain Geminus, 'who was that old woman at the docks?'

'Nobody. She came off a Cretan ship the week before. I put her up at the Grain and Grape, and paid her a few sesterces to act motherly at the docks.'

'She's not part of the ring?'

'No.'

'I trust you're telling the truth,' said Bato. 'If not, you and she will end up in the arena. Now tell us about Magnus.'

Zosimus sneered. 'Nobody has ever outwitted him, because he knows his enemies better than they know themselves. Information is his main weapon. That's why he pays me so well. You'll never catch him.'

'That remains to be seen,' said Bato quietly. 'Anything else you can tell us about Magnus?'

'Yes,' said Zosimus, and he began to giggle. 'He's a giant of a man.'

The next morning Nubia and her friends stood by the *Delphina*'s new stern ornament and watched Cnidos diminish behind them.

'It is a fair city,' said Nubia. 'The most beautiful I have seen.'

'And the people were nice, weren't they?' said Flavia.

Nubia nodded. 'They give us very many tasty food-stuffs,' she said, 'like dates.'

'And baby artichokes,' said Flavia. 'And fish and bread and lentils and onions.'

'And dolphin,' said Jonathan with a grin as Lupus patted the wooden dolphin that replaced the broken swan's neck.

'It's beautiful, isn't it?' said Flavia, stroking the dolphin's polished side.

'Yes,' said Nubia softly. 'It is magical. Now that we trade Zosimus for a dolphin,' she added, 'I think *Delphina* is happy at last.'

'Yes, now that we've traded Zosimus for this dolphin,' said Flavia, 'I think our voyage will get better.'

'You think?' said Jonathan. 'So far we've had falling yard-arms, galley fires, sulphurous whirlpools, runaway skiffs and freak storms.'

'Exactly,' said Flavia. 'Apart from killer whales or Tritons, I don't see how anything else could possibly go wrong.'

'It is like Land of White,' whispered Nubia.

'It even sounds white,' said Flavia. 'As if everything is muffled in wool.'

Lupus nodded.

It was the morning of the day before the full moon. They had woken on a damp deck to find their hair and fleeces soaked with moisture from a thick fog.

Jonathan looked around. The *Delphina*'s sails were limp and there was not even enough breeze to make her tackle clink. 'This is all your fault, Flavia,' he said with a sigh.

'My fault?' cried Flavia. 'Why is it my fault?'

'You said nothing else could go wrong.'

'You said *what*?' Captain Geminus appeared out of the mist. He wore his toga and had obviously been making an offering at the shrine.

'Um . . . nothing, pater,' said Flavia with a sheepish smile. 'I would never tempt the gods like that.'

'Just as well,' he said drily. 'But don't worry. Alexandros is convinced we're near Rhodes and Punicus says this fog should burn off by noon.'

But the fog remained all day and most of the following night.

'Great Neptune's beard,' whispered Nubia. The *Delphina* was gliding silently through a sea of mist. It was a breathtaking sight. With the yellow pre-dawn sky above and the mist swirling milky white just below the sails, the *Delphina* might have been sailing through the clouds.

Then Nubia lifted her gaze and saw something even more extraordinary.

Rising out of the fog bank before her were the peaks of an island.

On top of the highest, nearest peak stood the dark

shape of a temple and around it half a dozen figures, sharply silhouetted against the lemon-yellow sky.

Nubia made the sign against evil, for the silent sentinels were twice as tall as the temple. They were giants.

SCROLL XVIII

'They're statues, Nubia. Gigantic statues,' said Flavia.

'I know. But there are so many.'

Flavia nodded. 'Pliny says that in addition to the Colossus, there are over a hundred other enormous statues on Rhodes. There are statues of Aesculapius, Dionysus and Athena. But those statues on the ridge are probably Helios and his bride, the sea nymph Rhoda.'

'Which one is Colossus?' asked Nubia.

'Doesn't it straddle the harbour?' said Jonathan. 'With a leg on either side?'

'That's a common mistake people make,' said Flaccus, coming up behind them. 'The Colossus was never at the water's edge. It stood in the sanctuary, on the highest peak, but we can't see it from here because—'

'—it fell down in an earthquake!' cried Flavia. 'Pliny says so.'

Flaccus nodded and smiled, but Nubia was disappointed. She had imagined sailing underneath a giant bronze statue of the handsome sun god. In her mind's eye he looked just like Aristo.

Flaccus tossed his hair out of his eyes. 'Even lying on the ground the Colossus is still considered one of the

Seven Sights that must be seen. It's on that slope up there.'

'You've been to Rhodes before?' asked Flavia. She was standing on a coil of rope so that her head was level with his.

'No. But some of my friends have studied rhetoric here.'

A grunt from above made them all turn and look up. Lupus sat at the top of the mainmast. He was pointing straight ahead, towards the east. Suddenly he was flooded with golden light and Nubia stared at his illuminated figure floating above them.

Then the gold flowed slowly down the sail and lit the deck, for the sun had pushed its dazzling rim above the island, dissolving the mist with its light and warmth.

Tigris put his forepaws on the rail and looked forward with the rest of them, his nose testing the air. Presently they saw three separate harbours, filled with forests of masts. The lighthouse stood between the entrance of two of them and the *Delphina* steered for the smaller. Now Nubia could see the walls of the town, and the emerald slopes behind, dotted with enormous statues.

'Rhodes,' said Flaccus softly. 'The island of the sun.'

And Flavia quoted a verse from his poem, '*Arriving there is what you are destined for.*'

Nubia saw Flavia and Flaccus turn their heads to look at each other, and for a moment time seemed to stop. She had felt this once before, at the great amphitheatre in Rome. A sense of inevitability. That this moment was meant to happen. Then the feeling passed and like the others, she turned her gaze back towards Rhodes, the island of the sun.

'Maps, wind maps, guides to city and sanctuary! Buy them here!'

'Souvenirs! Painted flasks! Models of the Colossus!'

'Rhodian hardbake! Best in the Empire! Only ten sesterces a pack! Rhodian hardbake!'

Although it was only two hours past dawn, all the shops were open and many owners stood outside on the sunny pavement, inviting the Roman and Alexandrian tourists to look at their tapestries, rugs, leather goods, pottery, glass, jewellery or clothing.

Lupus stared around as they walked down the stone street towards the main square of Rhodes Town. They had berthed the *Delphina* at one of the town's harbours and Captain Geminus and his three-man crew were putting the first part of the plan into effect. Zetes and Tigris had stayed behind to help. Lupus and his friends – plus Bato and Flaccus – were executing a different part of the plan, and now Bato was leading them into a bright square with a splashing fountain at its centre.

'Yes, please!' A waiter in a spotless tunic stepped forward to intercept them. 'Just off the boat? Want breakfast?' he asked them in Latin. He obviously didn't mind their travel-stained tunics and dishevelled hair, for he gestured towards the tables of a tavern. 'We have figs, dates, yogurt, honey, cheese. Cinnamon rolls specialty of the house. Yes, please!'

Lupus's stomach growled and he looked at Bato.

'May as well,' said Bato. 'I'm ravenous. What do you think, Valerius?' he said to Flaccus.

'This one looks as good as any.' Flaccus pulled back two chairs in the shade for Flavia and Nubia, then sat beside Lupus in the bright morning sunshine.

Windchimes tinkled outside the shops as a gust of wind swirled through the square. The warm breeze rattled the fronds of the palm trees and whipped at the papyrus map Flaccus was unfolding.

'Where did you get that?' Flavia was sitting on his left.

'I bought it just now from that shop by the carpet-seller over there.' Flaccus pointed with his chin.

'Does it have the Street of the Coppersmiths marked?' she asked.

'Or show where the Colossus is?' asked Jonathan.

They all bent their heads to study Flaccus's map, then sat back as the waiter appeared with their drinks on a tray.

'Two hot spiced-wines, three mint teas and one buttermilk,' he said, placing this last before Lupus.

Their heads bent over the map again and Lupus pointed with a grunt.

'Yes,' said Bato. 'That's it. The Street of the Copper-smiths.' He lifted his head and looked around, then nodded towards an arch between the stalls of a silver-smith and a money changer. 'That street should take us there.'

'Useless!' said Flaccus, crumpling up the papyrus map and throwing it down onto the paving-stones in disgust. 'We'll never find the Street of the Coppersmiths!'

Bato shook his head and sighed. 'So much for the famous regular street-plan of Rhodes Town,' he said.

'Hark!' said Nubia. 'I think I am hearing the Street of the Coppersmiths.'

'She's right!' said Flavia. 'Listen.'

Above the cries of the swifts they all heard a faint tapping and tinkling.

Lupus had picked up the discarded map and was smoothing it out. Now he grunted and pointed towards the gloom of a covered alley.

'Yes,' said Nubia. 'Down this way.'

Gradually the metallic tapping grew louder and a moment later they emerged into a symphony of light and sound. The coppersmiths squatted beside their shop doorways, gripping the copper with hands and feet and tapping with little hammers. Braziers glowed red, sparks flew and the smell of charcoal drifted along the narrow street. The workmen – some no more than boys – were fashioning items like those which hung outside the shops.

Nubia stared at jugs, lamps, pots, pans, funnels, bells, windchimes, mirrors and trays. She saw round trays, square trays, oval trays, trays big enough to be table tops, trays small enough to be carried in the palm of one hand. The bright April sun beamed down onto the street, and its light bounced off the bronze and copper, throwing dancing lozenges of light on the buttermilk-coloured sandstone walls.

The shopfronts were just like those of Ostia, the same big rectangular doorways with their slatted wooden shutters rolled up for business. Each shop was a treasure cave inside, for the copper gleamed like gold. Nubia saw shelves of hairpins, thumb-rings, nose-rings, earrings, bangles, anklets, bells, beads, gaming counters, dice, manicure sets, bath sets, oil flasks, strigils, knives, votive animals and souvenirs. On a shelf just inside the big doorway of one shop she saw something which made her stop so abruptly that Flaccus trod on the back of her sandal.

Nubia reached out in wonder and picked up the little statuette. It showed a naked man holding a torch up high. On his head was a crown of sharp rays. She knew who he was because she had seen a similar statue before.

'Is this Colossus?' she whispered. 'It looks like statue in Rome.'

'Yes,' said Flaccus. 'Nero modelled his colossal statue on the one here in Rhodes.' He reached out to take another statuette from the same shelf and Nubia saw that there were dozens of them, all the same.

'Helios, the sun god,' said Jonathan. 'This must be what the Colossus looked like before it fell down.'

'Here's one of just its head,' said Flavia, stretching to reach a higher shelf.

'Yes, please!' said the plump shopkeeper in Latin, hurrying out from the dazzling depths of his cave. 'Don't touch! Childrens don't touch merchandise!'

He took the statuette from Nubia and set it back on the shelf with an artificial smile.

'I can pay,' said Bato, opening his coin purse and taking out some silver coins. 'How much would four of those cost?'

The shopkeeper's smile relaxed as he chose four small statuettes. 'These are best. For these I ask only thirty sesterces.'

'Fifteen sesterces,' said Bato. 'I can offer you fifteen.'

The shopkeeper shook his head sadly, feigning great regret. 'Most sorry but cannot ask less than twenty-five. Twenty-five sesterces.'

'Twenty,' said Bato, picking out five small silver

coins. 'Twenty sesterces *and*,' he lowered his voice, 'directions to the house of Magnus.'

Nubia saw the shopkeeper's smile fade instantly. He carefully replaced the four statuettes on the shelf and took a step back. 'No,' he said, holding up both hands apologetically. 'This I cannot do.'

Then he turned and scuttled back into the depths of his shop.

'For only two sesterces, *I* can tell you how to find Magnus,' piped a child's voice.

Lupus looked down to see a beggar-girl sitting on a greasy cushion with her back against the stone wall. The girl rattled a copper beaker containing two small bronze coins. She was grubby, with tangled hair, and she wore an oversized pink tunic that came down to her ankles. Lupus guessed she was a little younger than he was, perhaps eight years old. But there was something not quite right about her.

'Great Juno's peacock!' exclaimed Flavia. 'Where did you learn to speak Latin? Your accent is perfect.'

'In Rome,' said the girl, not looking at them. 'I come from Rome.'

She stood up and spat on the ground. 'I would show you where that scum Magnus lives for nothing,' she said, 'but I have not eaten for two days. So please give me something in return.'

Bato held out a silver denarius, worth four sesterces, but the girl did not take it. Then Lupus realised what was wrong.

The beggar-girl was blind.

★

'What is your name?' asked Flavia, as the little girl led them down the Street of the Coppersmiths.

'Mendusa,' said the girl, without turning her head. She held her cushion under one arm and wore her copper beaker on a string around her neck.

As they followed her, open shopfronts gave way to blank stone walls occasionally pierced by double doors and small high windows. What the doors led to, Flavia could not tell. Behind her, the metallic tapping and hammering of the coppersmiths grew fainter. Occasionally they passed a few people coming the other way, and Flavia noticed that most of the Rhodian men wore boots instead of sandals, and all the women covered their heads with their pallas.

'Mendusa,' said Bato presently. 'Can you tell us anything about Magnus?'

The blind girl stopped and put her finger to her lips. 'Is there an arch there?' She pointed to the right, just past a shop which sold copper lamps and lanterns.

'Yes,' whispered Flavia.

'Take my hand. Lead me there.'

Flavia led Mendusa through the arch, helping her to avoid a pile of donkey dung. The others followed them into a narrow side street that smelled of horse urine and leather.

'Don't try to fight Magnus,' Mendusa whispered. 'He is very clever. He speaks five languages and he always outwits his enemies.'

Bato and Flaccus exchanged a glance.

'Is he really a giant?' asked Flavia.

Mendusa nodded solemnly. 'He's eight, ten, maybe twelve feet tall.'

'How do you know?' asked Jonathan.

Mendusa turned her blank eyes towards him. 'I wasn't always blind.'

'What about the buyer in Asia?' asked Bato. 'In Halicarnassus. Do you know his name?'

Mendusa shook her head. 'Is that where they send them? At the carpet factory they said that if we were bad or tried to run away they would send us far away.' She groped for Flavia's hand and clutched it hard. 'I will tell you where to find him but promise you won't try to stop him. Nobody has ever succeeded. He is very dangerous and his spies are everywhere.'

'Just tell us where he lives,' said Bato gently. 'We have a plan.'

Mendusa reached out and patted the buttermilk-coloured stone. 'He is near. This wall is part of his very big house.'

'Good,' whispered Bato. 'Is there another way out of it? A back door?'

'Yes. Fifty paces down here and the first turning on this side.' She gestured with her cushion. 'There is a door. I do not know what colour it is but it is smooth all over, with no handle or knocker. You cannot get in, but people can get out.'

'Good,' said Bato and then, 'Flaccus, will you wait there, and follow anyone who comes out? Especially,' he added drily, 'any giants?'

Flaccus grinned. 'Of course.

'Wait!' said Flavia. 'We'll never find our way back here. We need a thread like Ariadne gave Theseus to help him find his way out of the maze.'

Lupus reached for his belt pouch but encountered only the leather sling that also served as a belt. They had left their belt pouches behind as part of their plan.

'What is it, Lupus?' said Jonathan. 'What were you thinking of?'

Lupus mimed drawing a gaming board on an imaginary table.

'Chalk!' said Jonathan. 'If we only had some chalk.'

Bato smiled and took a small wedge of chalk out of his own belt pouch. 'I like to play, too.' He broke it in half. 'Here, Flaccus. Take this. And remember: don't confront him, just follow him.' Bato turned to Flavia and her friends. 'Now, are you sure you're willing to do this?'

Lupus nodded.

'I'm sure,' said Jonathan.

'I also,' said Nubia.

'It was my plan,' said Flavia, though her mouth was dry and her heart thumping.

Bato looked at them for a moment with his pale eyes. 'Very well,' he said, taking a coil of rope from his canvas shoulder bag. 'Hold out your hands and let me tie you up.'

SCROLL XIX

Although they were only pretending to be captives, the feel of the rough hemp cord around Nubia's neck caused a choking wave of panic to fill her throat. She wanted to scream and run away, but she knew that she could not. It was Flavia's plan, and she had a part to play, so she breathed deeply and told her heart to be calm. She was doing this for the children.

Bato finished binding them and murmured something to Mendusa. The blind beggar-girl nodded and began to move down the Street of the Coppersmiths, her hand occasionally reaching out to caress the wall on her right. A group of chattering women further up the street disappeared through an arched opening, and as they walked past the closing door, Nubia heard female laughter and the spatter of an indoor fountain.

'That must be the women's baths,' Flavia whispered, and Mendusa nodded.

A moment later, the little blind girl stopped at a doorway. The lavender paint on the door was faded and peeling and the brass lion's head knocker green with age.

Mendusa groped for the lion's head knocker, then turned to them. 'This is it,' she whispered. 'Now I must go, or Magnus's men will find me and beat me. Be careful.'

'Goodbye, Mendusa,' whispered Nubia and Flavia. 'Thank you.'

But already the little blind girl was gone.

Bato gave a few sharp raps with the lion's head door knocker and presently they heard heavy footsteps.

Flavia swallowed and turned her head in order to loosen the cord around her neck; it felt too tight.

The door opened, but only a crack, and Bato spoke to someone Flavia could not see.

'My name is Titus Flavius Pharnaces,' said Bato, using the pseudonym they had agreed on earlier. 'I understand your master appreciates beautiful things. Please tell him I have some merchandise he might be interested in.'

The door opened a little wider and Flavia saw a big, sullen-looking man give them a rapid glance over Bato's shoulder. He nodded and the door closed again.

Silence.

They stood for a long time on the cobbled street in the bright sunshine, and Flavia heard the swifts shrieking above them and the faint tinkling song of the coppersmiths. Two women came down the street on their way to the baths, their laughter echoing off the stone walls, but when they saw Bato and the four children, they grew silent and pulled their pallas across their faces.

Flavia twisted her bound wrists – her hands were beginning to tingle – and it suddenly occurred to her that Bato could sell them for a fortune and flee to Asia before her father suspected anything was wrong.

Her heart began to pound, and she was trying to think how to tell Bato she had changed her mind, when the door opened and a veiled woman gestured for them to enter.

The woman wore a filmy tunic of scarlet silk over a rose pink shift. A magenta scarf covered all but her liquid black eyes. Her feet were bare but silver anklets jingled softly as she turned with a graceful gesture. They followed her through a dim vaulted vestibule and up half a dozen pink plaster-covered steps.

Flavia emerged into the scent of roses and the sound of pigeons. Into another world.

The sparkling white marble courtyard was planted with roses of every colour: scarlet, pink, white, yellow, cream. They were in full bloom and their petals carpeted the mosaic floor. As Flavia followed Bato and the slave-girl beneath a dovecote full of voluptuously cooing pigeons, the warm, sweet, heavy scent of roses almost made her swoon. It was a cube of paradise, and she wanted to linger there.

'Look!' whispered Nubia behind her. 'I see Achilles and Odysseus.'

A tug of the hemp cord around Flavia's neck pulled her out of the warm rose-drenched courtyard and along a shaded corridor towards gleaming marble stairs.

Just before they reached the stairs, a door on her right opened and another pink-veiled woman came out. The slave-girl quickly closed the door, but Flavia had caught a glimpse inside. The murmur of voices, the distinctive unpleasant smell of purple dye, and in the dim room a glimpse of looms with small shapes of children sitting before them.

And Flavia realised that this was not a paradise at all.

The cord around her neck drew her up the stairs,

through a door, into a cool, echoing, high-ceilinged room. Flavia's quick glance took in the pink marble walls, gauzy curtains, a woven carpet, a sandalwood screen, vases full of roses, silk floor cushions . . .

Her head swung back to the object at the centre of the room and she felt her jaw drop.

Through the diamond-shaped holes in the sandalwood screen loomed the shape of a man at least eight feet tall.

Jonathan sat on the carpet beside his friends and reminded himself that they were supposed to be playing the role of frightened children taken from the wreck of a ship called the *Delphina*. This was the scenario that would best fit with the recent storm and the messages carried by the pigeons.

'I am Magnus,' said the giant in a surprisingly light voice, 'Please be seated. And please excuse me for remaining behind this screen. I must retain my anonymity.'

Jonathan tried not to laugh. What was the point of an eight-foot giant keeping his face hidden?

'Tamar, give our guest some refreshment.'

The beautiful serving-girl moved silently to a low brass table and as she poured out a steaming liquid Jonathan smelled the familiar comforting scent of mint tea. Tamar set the small glass beaker on a copper tray beside a dish of green almonds and carried it to Bato, who sat cross-legged on the cushions.

Behind the sandalwood screen, the giant remained standing, and it occurred to Jonathan that he wanted to intimidate Bato with his size.

'Tell me,' said Magnus, when the serving-girl had

retreated, 'who are you and why have you come to see me?'

Bato cleared his throat. 'My name is Titus Flavius Pharnaces,' he lied. 'I'm a freedman, a banker. Until recently, I lived and worked in Neapolis. Last summer a volcano exploded. It killed almost all my debtors but it spared my creditors. Since then, life has become very difficult for me. I managed to pay my debts and scrape together enough money for the fare to Athens. From there, I found a boat to Cos, where I have a distant cousin named Timoleon, a fisherman. My cousin went out fishing two days ago and found these four children clinging to wreckage some distance from the coast.'

'Fascinating,' said Magnus. 'It sounds as if the children were victims of a shipwreck. Did your cousin see the remains of any ship?'

'No ship,' said Bato, 'but as Timo was rowing them back to shore he saw another man clinging to a floating mast. This man's injuries were much worse; he had lost his legs and was dying. Timo took him on board and the man said his name was Zosimus. Before he died, he told my cousin that if he took these children to a certain Magnus on Rhodes, he would be greatly rewarded.'

'Died, you say? This Zosimus died?'

'I'm afraid so. Timo and I burned his body on the beach and placed his ashes in an urn.'

Jonathan kept his eyes lowered. He knew that Zosimus was still alive in prison on Cnidos, awaiting trial.

'I hope this Zosimus was not a relative or close friend,' said Bato politely.

'He was a most useful client,' said Magnus from behind his screen, and then, 'Why did your cousin not come himself?'

'He's a humble fisherman. He has never travel-
led further than Symi to the south and Calymne to the
north. I was still in need of money, so I volunteered to
go.'

'And you realise these are freeborn children?'

'Yes, they have told me so repeatedly. You can see
that I had to strike one of them, the boy with the black
eye. Since then I've had no trouble.'

'Do you also realise that what you are proposing is
highly illegal?'

Bato lifted the small glass beaker and nodded, 'I hope
it will also be . . . rewarding,' he said carefully. 'For
both of us.'

'It will be,' said Magnus. 'Very rewarding. But first I
must tell you how I do business. I never barter. I will
make you an offer. You either accept or reject it.'

'Very well,' said Bato, taking a sip from the small
gilded glass.

'My offer is this,' came the voice behind the screen:
'Forty thousand sesterces for the lot.'

Bato almost choked on his mint tea. 'That's very
generous,' he said, putting down his glass and starting
to rise to his feet. 'I must consider your kind—'

'No,' said Magnus. 'Make your decision now. Either
keep the four children, or take the forty thousand. Once
you leave this place you will never return.'

Bato slowly sat down on the cushion and Jonathan
knew his mind must be racing.

In all their planning they had not foreseen this.

Bato had only brought the children here as a pretext
to see Magnus and the inside of the house. But how
could Bato take them away without arousing suspicion?
He had presented himself as a man desperate for

money, and here was someone offering him an enormous sum, far more than they had ever imagined.

'I can't accept less than a hundred,' said Bato at last. 'One hundred thousand sesterces.'

Jonathan heard the serving-girl stifle a gasp, and next to him Flavia stiffened. He himself was finding it hard to breathe. He knew Bato was taking a huge gamble. Magnus said he never bartered. By asking for one hundred thousand sesterces, Bato was showing himself to be greedy and arrogant. Magnus should now refuse, which would allow Bato and the children to leave without arousing suspicion.

But if Magnus had been bluffing – if he *was* open to barter – and willing to humble himself by giving in to this enormous demand, then Bato would have no choice but to leave them all behind in the clutches of this evil giant.

SCROLL XX

Magnus only paused for a moment, but to Nubia it felt like hours.

'I told you,' he said. 'I never barter. Tamar, please show our guest the way out.'

Bato rose.

'Oh, and by the way, Pharnaces . . .' said Magnus in a pleasant tone.

'Yes?' said Bato.

'If you come back for any reason, I will have you killed.'

Bato gave a stiff nod and as he turned to lead them out Nubia saw his face. Although it betrayed no emotion, it was as pale as parchment.

As the double doors closed, Flavia's trembling knees gave way and she almost fell down the marble stairs.

Bato caught her and jerked her roughly to her feet. 'Get up, you brat!' he shouted, giving her hand a secret squeeze. Flavia knew he was reminding her to play the role, so she let him shove her forward. Down the stairs, past the heavy door with its terrible secret, through the rose-filled courtyard, down more stairs, then under the vaulted ceiling of the vestibule and finally out through the double doors onto the sunlit street. Although she was only pretending to be a slave, she felt frightened and humiliated.

She turned her head and saw Nubia behind her, walking gravely and with dignity, and Flavia felt a sudden rush of affection for her friend.

'If Magnus is as brilliant as they say he is,' said Bato under his breath, 'one of his men will be following us right now. Keep pretending you're captured and frightened children.'

Flavia nodded. That wouldn't be hard.

At first Lupus couldn't see his ship among the others docked in the harbour. Then with a start, he recognised the hated black-and-yellow striped sail of the *Vespa*.

In just a few hours, Flavia's father and his crew had disguised the *Delphina*. Apart from replacing her old sail, they had taken away the sail from the front and they had painted a new image on the stern post – a wasp.

When Flavia's father saw them trudging up the gangplank, he ran forward.

'Don't hug me, pater!' Flavia hissed. 'Spies might be watching us!'

He nodded. 'Follow me,' he said in a low voice. 'I have something amazing to show you!' He disappeared down into the hold.

Bato untied their hands and pretended to shove them down the stairs. As Lupus's eyes adjusted to the dimness, he saw someone standing beside one of the water barrels. A big man with a good-looking face and bad teeth.

'Sextus!' cried Flavia, then clapped her hands over her mouth. 'We thought you were dead!'

'I thought so, too, Miss Flavia,' he said. 'When that

giant wave capsized our ship last summer, I thought I was going to Hades. But here I am in Rhodes.'

'Sextus has agreed to come back as a member of my crew,' said her father as he untied the rope around Flavia's neck. 'And he's told us where the *Medea* is. She docked three days ago in the eastern harbour, about half a mile away, and she's still in her berth.'

'Excellent,' said Bato, who was untying Lupus. 'Magnus's house is almost impregnable. It's hidden in a warren of alleys and has stone walls a foot thick. But if our information is correct, and he plans to transport some children tonight, then that's the perfect opportunity to catch him – while he's taking them from the house to the ship.'

'You could hide near the slave-ship *Medea*!' said Flavia. 'And then just as Magnus and his men are about to drive the children up the gangplank you could leap out and catch them!'

Lupus nodded.

'Precisely,' said Bato, moving on to Jonathan. 'Now that I have personally witnessed Magnus's illegal methods, I can go straight to the Roman governor of this province. I believe he lives in the house with the seven palm trees in front of it, the one we passed this morning, just inside the town gates. With his permission and a dozen of his soldiers, we should be able to overpower Magnus's men and free not only the children on the ship but also those left behind at the house.'

'Why hasn't the governor tried to stop Magnus before now?' asked Jonathan.

'I'm sure he has,' said Bato drily.

Captain Geminus had finished untying Flavia and her friends, and he was automatically coiling the cord which had bound them. 'Did you actually see the captive children at Magnus's house?' he asked.

'Yes,' said Flavia. 'I only caught a glimpse into a dark room but I saw some children sitting at looms. We saw Magnus, too. He's a giant.'

'A real giant?'

'At least eight feet tall,' came Flaccus's deep voice, and the light in the hold dimmed as he filled the hatchway. They all turned to watch him come down the stairs.

'Master!' cried Zetes and ran forward to kiss Flaccus's hand. 'Don't do that,' said Flaccus with an angry flush. 'You're freeborn, remember?'

Zetes hung his head and nodded.

'Quickly, Valerius,' said Bato to Flaccus, 'Tell us what you saw when you were waiting at the back entrance of Magnus's house.'

'About an hour after you left me – maybe less – the door opened and the giant came out. He was wearing a hooded cloak so I couldn't see what he looked like, just that he was huge. I'm almost six foot, but he was a good two feet taller. His hobnailed boots rang out on the cobbled streets and I was able to follow him for quite a while. I used your piece of chalk to scrawl a wavy "M" for Magnus on the walls. But then I lost him.' Flaccus moved forward and shook his head. 'He disappeared into a tavern. It wasn't very crowded but I couldn't see him anywhere. I'm near-sighted, but even so, I don't know how I could have missed a man that big. There wasn't even a back door. I hurried back out the front door, but by then he had gone. I'm sorry.'

'Never mind,' said Bato.

'We should go back to the tavern and look for secret tunnels,' said Flavia.

'Wait,' said Flaccus, 'there's more. When I was following Magnus I noticed some men painting a house. On my way back here I saw the same house, with the ladder leaning against it, but no workmen. So I borrowed it and followed my chalk marks back to Magnus's house. I was able to climb the ladder and look through some small high windows I had noticed earlier.'

'Did you see the children?' said Flavia.

Flaccus nodded. 'I saw them. When I looked in I must have blocked some light from the window. Every one of their heads turned to look up at me.'

'How many?' asked Bato.

'About fifty or sixty. I couldn't see very well, but I think some of them – maybe all of them – were chained to looms.'

'Great Neptune's beard!' cried Flavia's father. 'We must take action immediately. Sextus told us that the *Medea* is leaving tonight at an hour past moonrise.'

'Then you agree with my plan to enlist the governor's help and lie in wait by the *Medea*?' said Bato. 'And you'll help me?'

'Yes,' said Flavia's father.

'Yes,' said Flaccus.

'Yes,' said Sextus.

'Yes,' said Flavia, Jonathan and Nubia. Lupus and Zetes nodded too.

'NO!' said Bato and Flavia's father added, 'This is far too dangerous for children. You five must stay here on the ship with Sextus and promise not to interfere. If they plan to set sail an hour past moonrise, my guess is that they'll move the children under cover of dusk.'

Bato nodded. 'But we'll have to be in place well before then.'

'Oh, pater!' cried Flavia. 'You could be in danger!'

Captain Geminus nodded grimly. 'And that's why I want you to stay here. Sextus,' he added as they moved up the stairs, 'if we're not back by moonrise, alert the authorities.'

'This is called Monkey Harbour?' asked Nubia.

'That's what some of the locals call it,' said Sextus. He blew some wood shavings from the figurine he was whittling, a small deer.

It was late afternoon, the hottest time of the day. Because the air in the ship's hold had become unbearably stifling, Sextus had allowed them to crawl up on deck. The four friends and Zetes sat in the shade of the deckhouse, with their backs against the polished rail where they wouldn't be seen. The waxy smell of fresh paint was stronger up here, but there was a cooling breeze.

'Why do they call it Monkey Harbour?' asked Jonathan, who was searching for ticks in Tigris's fur.

'Is it because there are many monkeys on this island?' suggested Nubia hopefully.

'No monkeys,' said Sextus. 'But there are deer. Miniature deer.'

'I wish we could have gone with pater and Bato and Floppy,' said Flavia.

'Miniature deer?' said Nubia. 'Deer that are being most small?'

Sextus nodded. 'Many years ago there was a plague

of snakes here on Rhodes. That's why Rhodians wear boots and never sandals. The islanders tried every means to rid themselves of the plague, but nothing worked. There were snakes everywhere.'

Nubia shuddered.

'Finally,' said Sextus, 'they sent their wisest men to that famous oracle. You know, the one at Delphi. She told them to bring some little deer back with them. It worked. The deer sucked the snakes right out of their holes. Ate them all up.'

'I hate waiting and I hate not knowing what's happening,' said Flavia.

'Of all creatures, I do not like the snake,' said Nubia.

'Lupus doesn't like monkeys,' said Jonathan, 'Remember we got you a monkey for your last birthday? What a disaster that was!'

Lupus nodded.

'Have you seen the deer?' asked Nubia.

'Once or twice,' said Sextus. 'They live up there on the acropolis. The best time to see them is dawn or dusk. They often gather in the grove around the Temple of Apollo. They'll eat right out of the priestess's hand.'

Beside Nubia, Lupus stiffened.

'Have you seen the Colossus?' asked Zetes shyly. 'My master said he would take me to see it.'

'Of course I've seen the Colossus. One of his arms lies on the ground and there is a shiny band on the narrowest part of his thumb where men have tried to reach around it. Most men aren't big enough,' he added, 'but I am.'

'Where are you going, Lupus?' asked Jonathan.

Lupus stopped crawling towards the hatch-cover and

looked at them. Then he stuck his bottom in the air and mimed wiping it with a sponge-stick.

'More than I needed to know,' said Jonathan, and turned back to Sextus. 'Is it true that you can walk around inside the statue's legs and arms?'

'Yes,' said Sextus, 'but you have to be careful. The legs are still full of the huge rocks they used to keep it weighted down. Of course, that's just his thighs. The feet and lower legs are still standing.'

'The statue broke off at the knees, didn't it?' said Flavia.

'That's right.'

'I wonder if the legs fill up with water when it rains,' mused Jonathan.

'Then maybe ducks are swimming in his knees,' said Nubia.

'Sextus,' said Flavia presently. 'Please can you look and see if pater and the others are coming yet? The sun will be setting in less than an hour and I'm worried about them.'

Sextus sighed and stood up. 'By Castor! That little scamp!'

'What?' said Flavia. 'What is it, Sextus?'

'It's Lupus. He wasn't going to the latrine at all.'

Lupus had gone down into the hold but only long enough to put on his sandals. Then he had crawled across the deck and down the gangplank. Now his sandals slapped on the hot stone pier as he sprinted towards the town.

Apollo. There was a temple of Apollo with priest-esses up there on the acropolis. And his mother had made a solemn vow to that god.

The temple of Apollo on the acropolis of Rhodes: that's where his mother would be. He was sure of it.

Lupus slowed to a walk as the hillside grew steeper.

There were only a few people up here, coming down from the sanctuary. They were dwarfed by the colossal statues on either side of the path. The sun was low in the sky and it bathed the whole hillside in golden light. Further up the hill, twists of smoke rose from the evening sacrifices inside the sacred precinct.

The fallen Colossus was not visible from this angle – probably blocked by the theatre or one of the temples – but he could see a towering statue of Poseidon with his trident, and nearby a giant sea nymph or goddess. Lupus remembered that Poseidon was the father of the sea nymph Rhoda, after whom this island was named.

His heart began to pound as he caught sight of a colossal Apollo holding bow and arrows. But this Apollo stood on the exposed hillside, and there were no buildings near it. His temple must be the massive one right up there on the peak of the acropolis.

Presently Lupus stopped for a moment to catch his breath, then turned to look down. From up here he could see the whole of Rhodes Town spread below him, golden in the light of the setting sun. Further off he could see the lighthouse, its plume of dark smoke rising into the sky, and four of the five harbours, including Monkey Harbour. He could not distinguish his ship from the others and he wondered if Captain Geminus and Bato were back. Had they succeeded in freeing the children?

Then, as he turned to go back up he saw what he had not noticed before. An enormous full moon was rising in the east, to his right. If he looked straight towards the harbour, he could see both sun and moon in the sky together, one on his right, one on his left, one setting, one rising, but both above the horizon.

Was this a good omen, or a bad one?

Lupus turned and began to climb the marble steps that led up into the precinct itself. At the top of them a young priest stepped forward. His white robes were tinted orange by the sinking sun.

'I'm sorry,' he said politely. 'The sanctuary is closing for the evening. You can come back tomorrow. We open at dawn.'

SCROLL XXI

Lupus gazed around the sanctuary.

It had not been difficult for him to get in.

All he had needed was an ancient olive tree with twisted branches to help him up to the wall. He had run along the perfectly smooth marble top of the wall to another olive tree. The silver-grey leaves had trembled about him as he swung from one of the branches, then jumped lightly down. By staying low, and keeping behind the stadium, he had made it up the hill without being seen.

Now he had reached the end of the stadium. He needed to get to the temple of Apollo on the upper slope. The theatre and other temples up there would hide him, but to reach them he would have to cross open ground with nothing but a few rhododendron bushes to offer cover. He glanced around, listening, watching, using his intuition. There was nobody here. He could cross the open space.

But as he moved away from the stadium wall, he caught sight of something which made him stop and stare.

On his left – only twenty or thirty yards away – was an oak tree. And over it lay a fleece, sparkling gold in the light of the setting sun.

Lupus stood perfectly still and a shiver passed over him as he heard something like the faint tinkling of wind-chimes coming from the fleece which covered the oak tree. He rubbed his eyes hard, but when the little spots of light faded and his vision cleared, the fleece-covered tree was still there.

He moved towards it, drawn as if by some power. Then, at less than ten yards distance, he realised what it was.

It was a votive tree.

The oak wore thousands of rectangular leaf-thin scraps of copper on its branches, all with prayers inscribed upon them, each one probably offered with tears and vows. The votives were certainly dedicated to Aesculapius, for just beyond the tree stood a colossal statue of the Healer, and the sacred snake coiling up his staff was taller than the oak.

Now Lupus was close enough to touch the *ex votos*. He stood on tiptoe and reached up and held one of the trembling sheets of copper still so that he could read its Greek inscription: ASKLEPIOS PLEASE HEAL MY BABY PHYLLIA AND KEEP HER SAFE

He looked at some of the others. They all said similar things. Most were in Greek. But some were in Latin and some in alphabets that he had never met before. A glint of copper in the grass at his feet. He knelt and picked up a fallen *ex voto*. Someone had incised an eye on one side. The reverse was blank.

Lupus grunted and searched in the wildflower-dotted grass for a sharp stone. When he found one, he rested the rectangular sheet of copper against the tree's rough trunk and scratched a few words on its surface. He stretched to fold the scrap of metal leaf around one of the oak's lowest branches and bowed his head for a moment.

Then Lupus hurried on up the hill towards the grove of Apollo.

To you, O Helios, the people of Dorian Rhodes dedicate this bronze statue reaching to Olympus. May its burning torch of freedom shine over land and sea.

Lupus read the Greek inscription on the pedestal, then tipped his head back to see the two vast and trunkless legs of bronze, broken at the knees. He wondered what it must have looked like when it stood, visible for miles around holding its flaming torch high. The torch of freedom.

Nearby lay the massive left arm and hand of the statue. The huge fingers curved up away from the ground but the thumb lay close to the earth and a polished band showed where a hundred thousand visitors had tried to embrace it. To his right, part of the torso lay silhouetted like a small mountain against the pale lavender sky.

And on his left, further up the hillside and partly sunk into it, lay the enormous head of the fallen Colossus. The path up to Apollo's temple took him past it and he stopped for a moment to stare at the unseeing face of Helios the sun god and the massive bronze spikes which represented its rays. A shudder of awe passed through his body.

But he was not here to see the Colossus. He was here to find his mother.

Lupus moved round the colossal head, following a

well-trodden dirt path that led up to the ridge between rhododendron bushes.

Suddenly he froze. He heard the scuff of footsteps further up the hillside. Voices, too, coming closer: clear in the soft evening air. He did not want the priests to see him, so he stepped back behind a red-blossomed bush and waited for them to pass.

Two figures appeared in the dusk, moving down the path. They were not priests, but a man and boy, both wearing hooded capes. They passed so close that Lupus caught a whiff of rose-scented body oil and heard one of them say in Greek: '. . . to make sure he clears away all evidence of our existence.'

The light voice was familiar. He had heard that voice recently. This morning, in fact. His heart skipped a beat as he remembered Flavia's words: *Maybe it's a father and son team.*

Lupus looked up towards the sanctuary where his mother might be, then crept out from behind the large bush and started back down the path, almost slipping on some loose gravel as he approached the wicked spikes of the Colossus's head. Where were they? Had he lost them?

The path took Lupus round the statue's massive head and suddenly the breath was slammed out of him as he found himself held in the iron grip of a big man.

Magnus, the Colossus of Rhodes.

Lupus thrashed, trying to kick him, then bent his head to bite the forearm, but the arms squeezed tighter and now he couldn't breathe and the evening was darkening too fast. He stopped struggling and went limp. The arms relaxed a little and with a sob, Lupus filled his lungs with precious air.

As his vision cleared, Lupus saw the hooded boy standing a few paces away. The boy spoke. Not with the voice of a boy, but with the voice of a man. With Magnus's voice.

'Hello, Lupus,' he said. 'I thought I might find you up here. That's my bodyguard, Ursus. And my name – as I'm sure you know – is Magnus.'

The boy pulled back the hood of his cloak, and Lupus felt his jaw drop. He was staring at a man's head. A man's head on a body no bigger than his own.

Magnus was not a giant. Magnus was not a boy. Magnus was a dwarf.

'Sextus,' cried Flavia. 'We have to go to the authorities. Something has happened to pater and the others. I just know it. They should have been back by now. And Lupus might be in danger, too.'

'Your father told you to wait here.'

Flavia took a deep breath. 'He also told us to get help if they weren't back by moonrise. He said we should tell the authorities, remember? And look! There's the biggest moon I've ever seen rising behind the masts of those ships.'

Sextus shrugged. 'Get up, then. Let me put the rope around your necks in case Magnus's men are still watching this ship.'

'Oh thank you, Sextus! Bato said the governor's headquarters is on the way into town. It's the big yellow villa just inside the gate. The one with the palm trees in front.'

Sextus made sure the rope was securely round their necks and then said, 'I can't let you go.'

'What?'

'Sorry, Miss Flavia, but I can't let you go anywhere. I have to follow orders.'

'But . . . but those *were* pater's orders,' she spluttered. 'He told us to go and get help.'

'I said I had to follow orders.' Sextus pulled her hands roughly behind her back and began to bind them. 'I didn't say whose.'

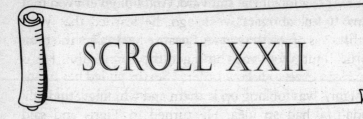

SCROLL XXII

'Ursus and I have just been up to the temple of Apollo,' said Magnus the dwarf, stepping forward until he was less than a yard away from Lupus. 'It's a beautiful temple. And attended by such lovely priestesses.'

Lupus stared.

'I asked them if they'd seen a young boy with no tongue. They said no, but one of them seemed greatly moved by my question. Zosimus told me you were devoted to your mother, Lupus. I'm surprised it's taken you so long to finally get here.'

Jonathan cursed as he realised they had been trapped. What good were all his new boxing skills if his wrists were bound tightly behind his back? Once again, he had let down those around him.

'Why are you doing this to us?' he asked angrily.

'Yes, Sextus, why?' Flavia's eyes filled with tears. 'You used to be our bodyguard. You protected us.'

'You saved the Pliny from drowning,' said Nubia.

'Why am I doing this?' said Sextus, now tying Zetes's hands. 'Money. Magnus pays good money, much more than your father gave me. Magnus is very important. He knows everyone in this town. When I first arrived here, he sent me a gift of a new tunic and sandals. He found me a job at the shipyard. And I'd never even met him. Then, about a week ago, he learned that your father was on his way here. Because he'd taken the time to find out about me, he made the connection. He is paying me very well.'

Tigris was looking up at them and whining. Suddenly Jonathan had an idea. He turned to Tigris and said loudly, 'Where's Lupus, Tigris! Go find Lupus!'

Tigris barked and wagged his tail and scampered across the deck, nose down, sniffing the deckhouse and hatch-cover, then hesitating at the side of the ship. Sextus lunged for the big puppy but Tigris was already running down the boarding plank.

'Where's Lupus?' shouted Jonathan again and then flinched as the furious Sextus loomed before him and brought back his massive arm.

The blow came with an explosion of bright shards behind his eyes and then he was falling . . . and he should have struck the deck by now but he was falling down and down and down into darkness.

Lupus was still gazing open-mouthed at Magnus. Even if he had been able to speak he would not have had any words.

'Go on, stare your fill,' said Magnus pleasantly. 'Ursus here has no tongue. Perhaps you should stare at him for a while, too. Still, I would have thought that you of all people would know what it feels like to be thought a freak.'

Lupus dropped his gaze in confusion.

'Oh yes, I know all about you. I make it my business to know my enemies, which is more than I can say for you and your friends. You didn't even know I was a dwarf, did you? I sit on the shoulders of Ursus here and they all think I'm a giant.' He laughed and then stopped. 'You were fools to imagine you could outwit me.'

Lupus raised his head angrily.

Magnus curled a lip. 'You sail into my port with a dolphin sail, then change it for a striped one. Did you really think that would fool anyone? Then you eat breakfast in the main square before pretending to be captured victims of a shipwreck? I'm not a fool. My people are everywhere. You can't trust anyone, Lupus.'

'Don't cry, Nubia. Jonathan's not dead. I think he's just unconscious. I know it looks hopeless, tied up like this in the hold of your old slave-ship, but pater will rescue us. He'll come charging in here with Bato and Floppy close behind, I just know he will. Or maybe Lupus will bring help. If Tigris can find Lupus then he'll know something's wrong. Oh please, Castor and Pollux, please save us!'

Lupus resisted the urge to hurl himself at the dwarf in fury. He was acutely aware of the fact that the more quietly he stood, the more Ursus relaxed his grip.

So he forced himself to stay calm as Magnus said, 'You're wondering if your friends succeeded, aren't you? Of course they didn't. I've taken care of Bato and Geminus, and that romantic poet. The *Medea* was just a decoy. She won't be sailing tonight. She served her purpose by leading the men into a trap. They'll find the ship full of my bravest fighters. As for your friend Jonathan and the girls,' he chuckled, 'and the beautiful Zetes, they will be part of tonight's delivery. Sadly, the last delivery ever,' he added, 'because I'm leaving Rhodes, and this time I'm taking all the children with me. By the way, Lupus, I must thank you for providing me with a new ship. We've loaded all the children on the *Delphina*. Or should I say the *Vespa*? She's a slave-ship again. After all, it's what she was built for.'

The rhythmic sound of clanking chains made Nubia's throat tighten involuntarily. She stared in horror at the children coming down the wooden stairs to join them in the *Delphina*'s hold. Most were thin and barefoot, dressed in ragged, greasy tunics. They were moving awkwardly, as if they had not walked for many months, and some of them were hunched like old men or women. Many were squinting and almost all were coughing.

'Nubia!' A boy was calling her name. 'Nubia!'

'Quiet, you!' came a harsh voice, along with the evil sound of a birch whip.

But Nubia had seen the boy who had called out her name.

'Porcius?' she whispered, and the boy nodded.

Nubia stared at Porcius in disbelief. The last time she had seen him in Ostia he had been a pudgy, self-confident boy who loved animals and kept mice for racing. He was thinner and paler, but what made him almost unrecognisable were the bruises and marks on his face. The left-hand side of his jaw was swollen and he had two spectacular black eyes.

Suddenly Nubia was furious. Furious with men who would beat an eleven-year-old boy, steal little girls from their parents, force children to make carpets against their will.

And she made a silent vow. From now on she would not be afraid. She would be angry.

Lupus had been standing quietly throughout Magnus's boasts because with each moment that passed Ursus unconsciously relaxed his grip a little more.

Suddenly, Lupus wrenched himself free of the big man's grasp and ran. He couldn't go down the hill, for Magnus stood directly in his path, so he ran back along the slope, dodging among the pieces of the fallen Colossus.

'Get him, Ursus!' he heard Magnus yell. 'Don't let him escape!'

Ursus was quick for such a big man, and the crunching hobnailed boots were coming up fast behind him. Lupus swerved and clambered into the gaping tunnel of the colossal arm. There was just enough light for him to see the places where the bronze had solidified in huge drips, like those on a wax candle. This was the inside, and never meant to be seen. The further he ran, the dimmer it became and once he stumbled on one of the drips of bronze. But he caught himself and ran on, for he could hear the ringing sound of hobnailed boots echoing in the vast bronze tunnel of the arm.

When he reached the colossal hand, Lupus used the bronze drips to help him climb up into it. Pausing for a heartbeat, he looked into the hollow interior of the hand, with the smaller tunnels of the curved fingers. There! One of the fingers had a hole in its tip, he could see the violet sky showing through. Was he small enough to squeeze through the hole? He'd have to try.

He turned quickly and backed into it on his stomach. Now he could see Ursus's running shape silhouetted against the opening at the far end of the arm. Behind him his feet felt for the opening. Now they were out in the cool evening air. He wormed his way back, felt his knees kicking in space and the bronze, cold and rough on his thighs. And now Ursus was there, grunting and stretching and straining, blocking what remained of the light. But Lupus had squirmed further back into the hollow space of the colossal finger, just beyond Ursus's reach.

Suddenly Lupus was out, dangling at arm's length from the statue's middle finger. He looked down and his stomach twisted. He was at least twelve feet above the ground. He remembered the time he had fallen from an umbrella pine in Ostia and he felt his mouth go dry. But he had no choice. He let go.

The fall jarred every bone in Lupus's body, and as he scrambled to his feet, he felt a stab of pain in his right ankle. He knew it wasn't broken but it twinged when he put his full weight on it. If he couldn't outrun Ursus he would have to fight him. There was not a moment to be lost. Even now Ursus would be charging back the way he had come, ready to resume the pursuit.

Lupus began to untie the knot in the leather belt around his waist. The belt could also serve as a sling. Already he heard the thump of Ursus's hobnailed boots as he jumped down from the far end of the arm. But where was Magnus? Quickly, quickly . . . Lupus's fumbling fingers could not undo the knot in his belt. There. It was free. He scanned the ground for a stone, snatched one up, fitted it into the pocket of the sling.

Now he could see Ursus coming straight towards him, charging along the dark bulk of the colossal arm.

Lupus had one chance. He could not afford to miss.

He quickly fitted the stone into the widest part of the belt and looped one end of the sling around the middle finger of his right hand. Then, holding the other end with the fingers of the same hand he whirled the sling until it hummed like a bee. Just pretend you're aiming at a seagull, he told himself. The trick was to visualise exactly where you wanted the stone to strike. Lupus imagined the stone striking Ursus right in the middle of his forehead. Then he let go of the sling's free end.

Ursus seemed to slam into an invisible wall, then he staggered backwards and sank onto the ground. Unconscious. Maybe even dead. Jonathan had once told Lupus that a big stone will knock people out but a small stone can kill them. But he didn't have time to check whether Ursus was dead or alive. And he didn't have time to look for another stone, because Magnus was coming up fast out of the dusk, his short arms swinging and his little legs pumping. The sight was almost comical, but Lupus did not laugh. Even in the deepening violet light Lupus saw the gleam in the dwarf's hand.

It was a dagger.

SCROLL XXIII

Gasping at the pain in his ankle, Lupus lurched towards the fallen head of the Colossus. He couldn't outrun Magnus. Maybe he could outclimb him.

The sun god's head had settled so deeply into the earth that some of its wickedly pointed rays and part of the neck were buried in the ground. But here at the back of the neck was a crack, and Lupus was able to pull himself onto the cold rough surface of the bronze. Now he was scrambling up onto the head, over the jaw and along the flat incline of the cheek. In the whorls of the colossal ear, he found a cavity deep enough to offer shelter for a few moments while he tied his belt around his waist again. Even if Magnus threw the knife it couldn't reach him here. But scuffing sounds told Lupus that Magnus was trying to follow him up onto the head.

Lupus peeked over the lobe of the ear. He had hoped the dwarf wouldn't be able to climb very well, but Magnus was coming up fast.

On his hands and knees now, Lupus scrambled out of the ear and away from Magnus. The massive bronze curls offered good hand-holds and presently he had reached the first slanting ray of the sun god's crown. The ray was almost as tall as the *Delphina*'s mast and up close its flat bronze surface was covered with a pitted crust of greenish metal. This patina gave Lupus's fingers something to grip and he made his way carefully around it to the next ray. The strap of his sandal was cutting into his swollen right ankle, so Lupus reached down, and started to loosen the thong. As he did so he leaned forward, peering from behind the ray.

There was Magnus, only a few feet away. The little man was moving straight for him.

Using the rough surface of the bronze, Lupus worked his way behind the second ray and peered around it.

Right into Magnus's face.

'Ahhhh!' shouted Lupus and lurched forward towards the next ray. He felt the dwarf's fingers brush his wrist and desperately writhed away. But his backwards step was clumsy and with a sickening flash of certainty he knew he was going to fall. As his sandalled foot slipped, he heard his own cry, felt the rough scrape of bronze on his thighs and chest, the wrench in his shoulders as his fingers found a grip on the statue's cold bronze curls.

He was dangling from the statue's hair. Looking down, he saw the smooth bronze forehead and below it a dizzying drop: not twelve feet, but more like twenty or thirty. Looking up, he saw an even more terrifying sight. Magnus, his handsome face gazing down at Lupus.

'This is better,' said the dwarf with a smile, 'We can make this look like an accident.' He slowly moved his right foot forward and Lupus felt the hobnailed boot press down on the fingers of his left hand.

Lupus gasped with pain and outrage. That was not fair!

Suddenly he had an idea.

He reached down with his right hand and undid the already loosened strap of his sandal. Then he flung the sandal at Magnus.

'Boh!' cried the dwarf as the sandal struck his wrist. The knife flew out of Magnus's hand and his arms flailed wildly as he tried to regain his balance. But his foot slipped on the same bronze curl and he pitched forward.

'Aiiieeee!' cried the dwarf as he tumbled past Lupus.

Heart pounding, Lupus pulled himself back up onto the hair of the Colossus and lay panting for a while. Presently he pushed himself up on his hands and knees and peered down.

Below him Magnus was struggling to his feet on a ledge formed by the sun god's nose.

'You little pest!' Magnus's face was in shadow but Lupus could hear the fury in the dwarf's voice. He was glad the dagger was out of play. Magnus was cursing now, trying to scramble up over one colossal eye back onto the crown of the statue's head.

Lupus hurriedly stood and limped back the way he had come, expecting the dwarf to tackle him at any moment. But as he slid back down the neck of the Colossus and eased himself to the ground it was not Magnus that knocked him over. It was something else.

'Oh,' groaned Jonathan. 'What happened?'

'Sextus betrayed us,' said Flavia's voice. 'He's working for Magnus and he knocked you unconscious. Are you all right?'

'No!' cried Jonathan. 'I can't see! I'm blind!'

'You're not blind. We're in the *Delphina*'s hold. They've shut us up here without lamps.'

'What's that coughing and whimpering?'

'There are about sixty children in here with us. They've loaded them on this ship, not the *Medea*.'

'What's your plan to get us all out of here?'

Silence.

'You do have a plan don't you?'

'Well, we think there are only two guards plus Sextus. They're up on deck.'

'Only three guards for sixty prisoners?'

'Jonathan, you should see them. Even if they didn't have chains around their necks, most of them couldn't run. Some of them can barely walk.'

'I thought Magnus only shipped out the pretty ones.'

'Not this time, I guess. But Jonathan, we're the only ones tied with rope and I think I've almost untied Nubia's hands. It's just hard—' he heard Flavia grunt '—to untie a rope backwards in the dark.'

Jonathan felt a stab of dread. 'Tigris!' he cried. 'Did he get away?'

'Yes,' said Flavia, 'but it's been a long time now. I hope he's all right.'

'Arrrgh!' grunted Lupus, pushing the creature away. Something had pinned him to the ground. Something with a hot tongue and doggy breath.

Then he laughed with relief as he saw Tigris's panting face looming over him. The big puppy's tail was a blur in the moonlight and as Lupus staggered to his feet Tigris leapt up, too, and tried to lick his face.

As Lupus patted Jonathan's dog, an idea dawned in his mind.

Hooking his finger in Tigris's collar, he limped round to the front of the enormous bronze head and pointed up at Magnus, who was trying a different route down from the colossal nose. When the dwarf saw Tigris, he scrambled back up onto the nose and glared down. Tigris was not even a year old, but his father had been a mastiff and he was already bigger than most full-grown dogs.

Lupus pointed to Magnus and then growled fiercely. Tigris looked up at Magnus and then at Lupus. Lupus growled up at Magnus again. Tigris growled at Magnus and Lupus patted the dog's head. Then he gently pushed Tigris's bottom, making him sit. But when Lupus started to limp back down the path towards the harbour, Tigris rose and began to follow him.

Lupus patiently led Tigris back to the same spot, made him sit and uttered a commanding grunt. This time Tigris understood. He turned his head and whined as Lupus backed off, but he did not leave his post.

'Well played, Lupus!' came Magnus's light voice. 'You win. Just call off your mastiff. I need to get down to the harbour now.'

Lupus ignored him and started down the path. The moon was rising steadily and the ship – his ship! – would sail within the hour. He didn't have much time.

'Melissa!' The dwarf's cry brought Lupus up short. 'Your mother's name is Melissa, isn't it?'

Lupus turned, his heart pounding. Magnus was still standing on the ledge of the sun god's nose. He jerked his little arm up towards the grove.

'She's up there now. At the temple of Apollo. I've just seen her. Your uncle often spoke of her but I wanted to see for myself. I wanted to see her beauty before she died.'

Lupus's feet – one sandalled, one bare – took him back up the hill. Beside the path something caught his eye. Magnus's dagger, gleaming in the moonlight. He bent, picked it up, slipped it into his belt, almost without thinking. Then he looked up at Magnus. The moonlight showed the dwarf's handsome features and Lupus saw him smile. Was he dreaming? Was this some nightmare?

'I know about the vow she made,' Magnus spoke so softly that Lupus had to come even closer. Tigris wagged his tail but Lupus kept his eyes on the dwarf.

'Zosimus wrote to me,' said Magnus. 'He told me how devastated you were when you heard she had left Symi. So I took the time to find her, because I must know everything about my enemies.'

Lupus took a step closer and Tigris whined softly.

'You know, Lupus, a few months ago, when I first heard that you killed one of my best agents, and that you had somehow acquired his ship, I knew I had made a powerful new enemy. Others might underestimate you but I would not. And I was right. Nothing I did seemed to stop you from coming here to Rhodes. That's why I had to resort to finding your mother. Did you know she promised to sacrifice her life to Apollo if you survived? That was the vow she made and she's about to fulfil it. The priest was sharpening the knife when I left.'

Lupus tried to cry out 'No!' but it came out as a groan.

Magnus pointed dramatically towards the east. 'That full moon is her executioner, Lupus. As soon as it rose they began the ceremony. So call off your hound and go to her. If you hurry, you might be in time to save her.'

Lupus shook his head, trying to clear it. Except in Greek plays, he had never heard of the gods demanding human sacrifice. Was his mother really about to die on the altar of Apollo? Or was this Magnus's bluff to keep him away from the *Delphina*?

Once the *Delphina* left the harbour, Magnus would be safe. There would be no evidence to convict him. The captured children would be gone forever, absorbed into the vast continent of Asia to become slaves, or worse. And his friends would disappear along with them.

Lupus clearly remembered the first time he had seen Flavia, Jonathan and Nubia – three very different-looking children standing around his bed in the lamp-light, looking at him with concern. They had accepted him and befriended him. They had laughed together, played music together, solved mysteries together. And one magical night the four of them had swum with dolphins. How could he abandon them?

But his mother. His *mother*. They might be killing her now. How could he abandon her?

The ground was tipping and tilting like the deck of a ship. He felt sick and found himself on his knees, his forehead pressed against the cool dust, his breath coming in panting gasps.

He had a terrible choice. He could save his friends or he could save his mother. He couldn't do both. God, please help me, he prayed.

Instantly he heard a voice in his head say: *You made a vow*.

Suddenly everything was clear. He knew what he

had to do. Lupus stood on trembling legs and breathed deeply.

'Run!' Magnus was saying. 'If you run you might be in time.'

Lupus kicked off his remaining sandal and although his ankle still hurt like Hades, he ran.

SCROLL XXIV

Flavia still hadn't managed to untie Nubia, and the hope was dying in her heart when she heard an enormous thud and then scuffling on the deck above.

Muffled shouts and curses, more echoing thuds, and then the quick rhythmic stamp of feet which must be a line of soldiers. Finally the sound of the hatch-cover being opened and her father's wonderful voice calling 'Flavia? Are you there? Flavia?'

'Yes, pater!' she cried. 'We're all down here! Help us!'

All eyes turned towards the stairs as a flickering light appeared and a boy limped down into the dim hold.

'Lupus!' cried Flavia, Jonathan and Nubia together.

Flavia saw his eyes widen as he looked around at all the children. Then a man's legs appeared behind him, and a tunic with a narrow stripe on each side which Flavia recognised with a sob of relief. 'Oh, pater! We thought they'd killed you!'

'No, my little owl,' he said, but his smile faded as he held out his swinging oil-lamp and saw the children – emaciated, filthy, and terrified – huddling among amphoras and sacks of salt. 'By all the gods!' he muttered, 'when I get my hands on that miserable dwarf . . . Flaccus, would you help me get these children out of their bonds and up on deck.'

'Master!' cried Zetes, and Flavia saw Flaccus coming down into the light. There was blood on his tunic and an ugly gash by one of his dark eyebrows. He scanned the dim faces in the hold and his handsome face relaxed into a smile as he saw Zetes.

'Where's Bato?' Flavia asked her father. 'Is he all right?'

'Yes. Thanks to Flaccus's skill as a boxer. Bato's up on deck, helping the authorities.'

'Pater!' cried Flavia. 'Sextus is up on deck, too! He betrayed us! Don't let him go!'

'I know. He attacked us, but Flaccus knocked him cold.' Her father had been picking his way carefully through the whimpering children and now at last he reached her. He hung the oil-lamp from a hook on the beam above and gave her a quick, fierce hug. Then he began to cut the rope around her neck. Flaccus was beside her, too, cutting Zetes free with a knife.

'What happened pater?' asked Flavia. 'Did you find Magnus?'

'It was a trap,' said her father grimly, loosening the loop around Nubia's neck, before cutting it. 'The little blind girl was working for Magnus. So was the waiter who served us breakfast this morning, and some of the coppersmiths. It seems half the people on this island receive money and favours from him. Lupus was clever to remember where the governor lived, and to find him. If he hadn't come with reinforcements we would be dead.'

'Lupus,' said Jonathan, keeping his head still as Flaccus cut away the rope collar. 'You saved us!'

Lupus looked up at Jonathan with a strange bleak expression on his face.

'Lupus saved us all,' said Flavia's father. 'Apparently he trapped Magnus and his bodyguard up on the acropolis long enough for us to—'

'Magnus has a bodyguard?' asked Flavia, as her father started on the knot tying her hands.

'Magnus is a dwarf,' explained Flaccus. 'He rides on the shoulders of his bodyguard, a big thug called Ursus, a mute. But if you see them together you think they're father and son. That's why I didn't recognise him in the tavern.'

Flavia's hands were free now and she threw her arms around her father. 'Oh, pater!' She felt hot tears filling her eyes. 'We were so frightened and – of course!' she cried, pushing away from her father and looking up at Flaccus. 'Magnus is a dwarf! That's why they call him both Hector and Astyanax. Magnus is like Astyanax and the big thug is Hector.'

'And Magnus rides on the shoulders of his mute bodyguard,' said Jonathan, 'just like Astyanax rode on the shoulders of Hector when they were fleeing Troy.'

'That was Anchises, not Astyanax,' said Flavia and Flaccus at the same moment, and smiled at each other.

'What is mute?' asked Nubia.

'It means he can't speak,' said Flavia's father. 'He had his tongue cut out, like Lupus.'

'How did you trap him, Lupus?' asked Flavia, and then 'Lupus?'

But Lupus had gone.

The moon was directly above by the time he reached the colossal head.

There was nobody there. No Magnus. No Ursus. No Tigris. Just the huge head, eerie in the silver moonlight which cast the lower side of its face into inky shadows. The words of a poem – he could not remember which one – came into his mind: *The rock that toppled the statue became a huge mountain and filled the earth.*

For a moment Lupus gazed at the head with its unseeing eyes, then he limped up the moonlit path between dark rhododendron bushes. No point hurrying. The ceremony would be over by now. And he dreaded what he might find.

The path became marble stairs and his legs grew heavier with each step. Presently he reached the temple of Apollo. A huge dark cube surrounded by silent figures so vast that they blocked out the stars. Colossal statues. Like gods frozen with horror at what they had seen.

Before the temple stood an altar, still glowing red with embers. He caught the nauseating sweet smell of burnt meat, and was almost sick. Then he recognised the smell of mutton and his racing heart beat a little slower.

He did not hear the nightingale trill, or feel the warm night breeze ruffle his tunic, or see the tiny white stars of fireflies blinking among the rhododendron bushes. But something drew him past the altar towards the inky black pine grove beyond. And presently he reached a moonlit clearing with the marble statue of a robed woman at its centre.

He froze. Three tiny deer were approaching the statue. Then the statue moved and Lupus saw it was a woman: a priestess with her head covered by her white palla. One of the tiny deer took some food from her outstretched hand.

His heart was pounding violently again. Was it his

mother? He stepped out of the shadows and into the moonlight.

All three deer froze – their small heads and big ears turned towards him – then they bounded off into the woods and only the woman remained. The priestess turned and pulled back her head covering to reveal white hair.

Lupus's heart sank and his shoulders slumped.

The priestess smiled. 'You have come to find your mother, haven't you?' she said softly in Greek.

He nodded, and saw tears shining in her eyes.

'I'm sorry, Lukos, but you are too late.'

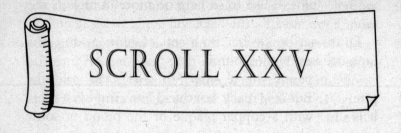

Is SHE DEAD? Lupus's finger trembled as he wrote in the cool dust at the foot of a pine tree.

'Yes,' said the priestess with a sad smile, 'and no. Once you take a vow to Apollo you are dead to your old life. Devoted to the god alone.'

Lupus tried not to sob with relief. He closed his eyes and offered up a brief prayer of thanks. Then he wrote: IS SHE HERE?

The priestess paused and glanced away. 'No. She has gone to another sanctuary of Apollo.' She turned her gentle gaze on Lupus again. 'But even if she was here, I would not be allowed to tell you. Nor would you be permitted to see her. She has been sanctified. Set apart. I will explain it to you. Come with me.'

The priestess led him silently back to the clearing in front of the temple. She took a ceramic beaker from a niche behind the altar, and lifted a bronze jug from the coals on top and poured a draught of steaming liquid. From the smell he guessed it was spiced wine mixed with milk. But there was another scent, faint but familiar, that he could not place.

'Drink this,' said the priestess. 'It will calm your heart.'

When he had drunk, she led him to the foot of a tall

umbrella pine. 'I like to sit here on moonlit nights,' she said. 'If we are still, the deer will come to us again.'

Lupus sat beside her on a soft cushion of dust and pine needles. He felt numb.

'Many people make vows to the gods,' said the priestess. 'But few really honour them. And even then, it is only with a copper plaque or the blood of some poor animal.'

Lupus leaned his head back against the rough bark of the tree and closed his eyes.

'Only a few people,' said the priestess, 'make truly heroic vows. When you were torn from your mother's arms, when she saw that man cut out your tongue and take you away, she made such a vow. She promised Apollo that if he preserved your life, then she would give him hers in return. Like a sacrifice. But not a sacrifice of death. A sacrifice of life. Your mother will serve the god in one of his sanctuaries for the rest of her days. She will live well as the priestess of Apollo. She will have food and drink and a soft bed. They will teach her to serve and pray and prophesy. And she will gain the respect of both men and gods.'

Lupus opened his eyes angrily and pointed at himself, as if to say, 'But I am here now!'

'I'm sorry, Lukos. If we had known that you were in Rhodes we would have delayed the ceremony. But now that she has begun she must continue. The vow is very solemn and must be honoured. Can you understand that? Just a little?'

Lupus felt the anger drain away. He nodded. He understood because he had made a heroic vow, too.

Not the vow on the beach, which he had sanctified with pigeon's blood, and repeated on board the *Delphina*, but a vow which no person had heard, no copper plate had recorded, no blood had solemnised. It was a vow made in his heart.

In the colossal amphitheatre at Rome, one month before, when it seemed as if Jonathan must surely die, he had prayed to Jonathan's god, vowing that if he would save Jonathan, he would give his life in return. Lupus felt that of all the vows he had ever made, that one alone had been heard and recorded.

He suddenly realised that he and his mother had made similar vows. Only for different people. And to different gods. Jonathan's god no longer had a temple or sanctuary, and Lupus wasn't sure how to serve him. But one thing he did know: the voice he had heard in the skiff had been real. As real as the voice at the colossal head a few hours before. He had to honour his vow just as surely as his mother had to honour hers.

He looked at the priestess. She held his gaze for a moment and her eyes widened. 'You do understand!' she said softly.

Lupus nodded. Yes, he understood. But that didn't make it hurt any less, and he felt the tears come in a hot flood.

He wept for a long time, and the priestess sat quietly beside him. The moon had dropped behind the treetops and now it was dark, but the night was still velvet warm and filled with fireflies. There must have been something like poppy tears in the tonic she had given him, for now his eyelids felt very heavy and finally he let them close.

He heard the soft rustle of the priestess's robe as she stood, and whispering feminine voices and then someone else sat beside him there at the base of the tree. And now he could feel soft arms around him and he smelled honey and he heard a sweet familiar voice singing the words of a half-remembered lullaby: *When you come home, when you come home to me.*

He wanted to see her – just to remind himself of what she looked like – and so he tried to open his eyes. But his eyelids were far too heavy and perhaps it was only a dream after all.

Lupus settled himself into his mother's arms, and presently he slept.

When Lupus woke at the foot of an umbrella pine, lying on ground felted with dust and pine needles, he thought at first that he was still a beggar-boy sleeping rough in Ostia's graveyard.

He felt the warmth of a soft garment over his shoulders and caught a whiff of incense, but it was not until he turned his head and saw the pure brilliant light filling the sky above him that he remembered he was in Greece.

The white-haired priestess smiled at him from the altar and in the sunshine he could see that although her hair was white her face was hardly lined. She moved forward and kissed his forehead and asked him if he would like to have breakfast with her. He shook his head and wrote in the dust, telling her that he had to go back to his friends. The priestess smiled and asked if by chance one of them was a dwarf, a very handsome dwarf?

'I'm sorry, Lupus,' said Flavia later that morning. 'Magnus got away. Ursus, too. They were gone by the time the soldiers reached the Colossus. Bato thinks they've escaped to Asia.'

Lupus had just returned and the four friends were sitting at the table on the sunny deck of his ship. The *Delphina* was still berthed in Monkey Harbour but she wore her dolphin sail once more.

'Tigris returns last night just after you depart,' said Nubia.

'If only you could talk,' said Jonathan, stroking Tigris. 'You could tell us how Magnus got away.'

'But you were a good dog,' said Flavia. 'You saved Lupus and he saved us.' Tigris thumped his tail and Flavia craned her neck to see what Lupus was writing on his wax tablet.

WHERE ARE ALL THE CHILDREN?

Flavia pointed. 'See that ship moored over there? The one with the red stripe round her hull? She's the *Medea*. That's where they are.'

They all laughed at the expression on Lupus's face and Flavia explained, 'Bato confiscated the *Medea* and he's taken all the children on board. He's going to take them back to their families in Ostia as soon as possible.'

FLACCUS TOO? wrote Lupus.

'I'm not sure where Floppy is going from here,' said Flavia.

'Halicarnassus,' said a deep voice and she turned to see Flaccus. He looked very handsome in a clean tunic and dark grey travelling cloak. The cut over his left eyebrow was barely visible. 'I'm going on to Halicarnassus,' he said.

'You mean you're just going to continue your tour of the seven sights?' she said, and added coldly, 'I suppose the Mausoleum is next on your list?'

'Yes,' he said, with an amused smile. 'It's the perfect excuse to go to Halicarnassus. Nobody will suspect that I'm really trying to find a criminal mastermind. They'll all assume I'm a spoilt patrician poet with nothing better to do than see the Seven Wonders.' He looked pointedly at Flavia as he said this and she felt her face grow hot.

Then she realised what he had just said.

'You mean you're secretly going to track down Magnus and Ursus, and find out where the other children were taken?'

He nodded. 'All my life I've felt sorry for myself because of my disability – my shortsightedness. I'm always insulting important men by not recognising them in the forum or by ignoring their smiles, simply because I can't see them. And I've often wondered how I can plead a case if I can't see the jurors' expressions. But this is something I can do that will make a difference. And it might help balance the scales as far as Zetes is concerned.'

'Will Zetes go with you?' asked Nubia.

'No,' said Flaccus. 'He's going back to Italia with Bato. It wouldn't be right for him to serve me any more.' Here he turned to Flavia. 'And I want to do what's right,' he said softly, with a look that made her stomach do a strange flip.

'Euge!' she laughed. 'Floppy is going to help find the missing children!'

The others laughed, too, and Flaccus smiled at Flavia. Two weeks at sea had deepened his tan and his teeth were very white. 'There's just one thing I'd like you to do for me, Flavia.'

'Yes?' Her heart was beating hard for some reason.

'Please call me Gaius. I really do hate being called Floppy.'

Three days later, high on the acropolis of Rhodes, a priestess with honey-coloured hair looked down on the town and the harbour beyond.

A ship was moving slowly out through the columns that marked the entrance of Monkey Harbour. It disappeared for a moment behind the lighthouse, then reappeared on the open sea. As she watched, the white sail unfolded and filled and when she blinked away the tears, she could just make out a tiny leaping dolphin painted there.

The sky was blue from rim to rim, a vast bowl filled with sunlight and the joyful cries of wheeling swifts. She lifted her face to the sun and let its golden warmth caress her and she asked Apollo to protect the dolphin ship and all those who sailed in it, especially its young owner.

When she opened her eyes again, the ship was just a notch on the horizon.

Lupus clung to the foremast and looked down at the blue-green water rushing past. The glittering light on its surface dazzled his eyes. The sun was warm on his back and he could feel the living urgency of the *Delphina* as she rose and fell beneath him. They were sailing towards Athens, Corinth and Ithaca.

The words of Flaccus's poem came into his head: *Always keep Ithaca in mind. Arriving there is what you are destined for.*

Lupus lifted his face to the wind and breathed the sea-smell deep in. Another verse came to him, the words clear in his head: *The Sirens and the Harpies, and even the Cyclops hold no danger for you. You won't find monsters, unless you erect altars to them in your heart.*

Lupus wondered, How did you erect altars to monsters?

The answer came almost at once: By thinking about them, by hating them, by vowing revenge.

Once before, Lupus had rid himself of the monsters, but now he realised that he had erected new altars to them.

He closed his eyes and prayed, and as he prayed he saw that the monsters were no more than statues of sand on the shore. In his mind's eye he let the waves of the sea melt Venalicius the Cyclops, Zosimus the Traitor and Magnus the Colossus. He let the sea wash away every bit of anger, fear and guilt. It was surprisingly easy.

He realised he was weeping, which was strange. Because now his heart felt cleaner and smoother than the beach on which he and his childhood friends had played. There were no monsters there. No altars. Only a man, asking if he could take the helm of Lupus's ship. Lupus gave a small nod and hugged the *Delphina*'s polished foremast.

He thought of the cargo in her wooden belly: Corinthian bronzes, Calymnian honey, sponges from Symi, rose-scented oil and mastic-flavoured hardbake from Rhodes. Such treasures would easily restore Captain Geminus's fortunes. And there was another treasure on board, a much more precious treasure: people who loved him.

Another verse from the song came into his head. *Pray that the voyage will be a long one, with many a summer's evening when you enter harbours you have never seen before.*

Lupus knew that one day in a sanctuary near some harbour he would find his mother again. Meanwhile there were many places for him to visit. New lands, new skies, new adventures. He had a destiny now, and someone trustworthy to guide him.

And somewhere along the way, he would discover what Ithaca meant.

FINIS

ARISTO'S SCROLL

Acastus (uh-*kast*-uss)
mythological son of Pelias (Jason's uncle and enemy); he was one of the argonauts

Achilles (uh-*kill*-eez)
Greek hero: a fast runner and the greatest warrior of the Trojan War

Acrocorinth (uh-*krok*-oh-rinth)
the dramatic sugarloaf mountain that rises above Corinth; site of a sanctuary and notorious temple of Aphrodite attended by beautiful priestesses

acropolis (uh-*krop*-oh-liss)
literally: 'highest point of a town', usually the site of temples and sanctuaries and very often fortified with thick walls for defensive purposes

Aegean (uh-*jee*-un)
sea between modern Greece and Turkey north of Cnidos

Aeneid (uh-*nee*-id)
long poem by the Roman poet Virgil about the Trojan hero Aeneas

Aesculapius (eye-skew-*lape*-ee-uss)
(Greek Asklepios) son of Apollo and Coronis, he was the god of healing

Africus (*aff*-rick-uss)

wind from the south (strictly south south-west) which often brings stormy seas

Agamemnon (ag-uh-*mem*-non)

King of Mycenae and leader of the Greeks who sailed to fight against Troy

Alexandria (al-ex-*and*-ree-ah)

port of Egypt and one of the greatest cities of the ancient world

altar

a flat-topped block, usually of stone, for making an offering to a god or goddess; often inscribed, they could be big (for temples) or small (for personal vows)

amphitheatre (*am*-fee-theatre)

an oval-shaped stadium for watching gladiator shows, beast fights and executions; the Flavian amphitheatre in Rome (the 'Colosseum') is the most famous one

amphora (*am*-for-uh)

large clay storage jar for holding wine, oil or grain

Anchises (ank-*eye*-zeez)

old, lame Trojan loved by Venus in his youth, his son Aeneas carried him on his shoulders as they fled from burning Troy

Anthemoessa (anth-em-oh-*ess*-uh)

literally 'flowery'; island of the Sirens in the Tyrrhenian Sea, modern Capri

Aphrodite (af-fro-*dye*-tee)

The Greek goddess of love; her Roman equivalent is Venus

Apollo (uh-*pol*-oh)

Apollo was god of the sun whereas Helios (see below)

was the Titan who drove the sun across the sky in a
chariot

Apollonius Rhodius (apple-*oh*-nee-uss *road*-ee-uss)

poet from Alexandria who wrote the *Argonautica* in the
late third century BC

apotropaic (ap-oh-tro-*pay*-ick)

having the power to avert bad luck or evil

Aramaic (air-uh-*may*-ik)

closely related to Hebrew, it was the common language
of the first century Jews

Argo (*arr*-go)

Jason's famous oared-ship, named after its old builder,
Argus

argonaut (*arr*-go-not)

any one of the mythological heroes who sailed with Jason
on the *Argo*

Argonautica (arr-go-*not*-ick-uh)

story of Jason's search on his ship *Argo* for the golden
fleece; the most famous version was written by
Apollonius Rhodius in the late third century BC

Argus (*arr*-guss)

mythological ship-builder who built the *Argo* for Jason; he
was one of the argonauts

artemon (*art*-em-on)

sail at the front of the ship on the foremast; used from the
first century AD

Asia (*aze*-ya)

Roman province which included Rhodes and its
surrounding islands, and much of modern Turkey

Astyanax (as-*sty*-an-ax)

infant son of the Trojan hero Hector

Atalanta (at-uh-*lan*-ta)

   mythological girl who could run faster than any man;
   according to some ancient versions she was one of Jason's
   argonauts

aulos (*owl*-oss)

   wind instrument with double pipes and reeds that made a
   buzzy sound

barbiton (*bar*-bi-ton)

   a kind of Greek bass lyre, but there is no evidence for a
   'Syrian' bass barbiton

Berenice (bare-uh-*neece*)

   beautiful Jewish Queen who was Titus's lover in the AD
   70s

brails (braylz)

   ropes attached to the bottom of a sail, running over the
   front of the sail to the yard and then back down; by
   pulling the brails you could raise the sail, like blinds

brazier (*bray*-zher)

   coal-filled metal bowl on legs, like an ancient radiator

Calymne (*kal*-im-nay)

   (modern Kalymnos) island near Rhodes famous for its
   honey and sponge-divers

Caprea (kuh-*pray*-uh)

   (or Capreae) modern Capri, a beautiful island off the
   coast of Italy near Sorrento; traditionally the haunt of the
   Sirens

Caria (*care*-ee-uh)

   southern mainland region in the province of Asia
   (modern Turkey) near Rhodes

Castor (*kass*-tur)

   the mortal one of the mythological twins, the Gemini,

who sometimes appeared as eerie blue lights on ships'
rigging, a phenomenon now known as St Elmo's fire

Cenchrea (ken-*cree*-uh)

Corinth's eastern harbour; one end of the *diolkos* was
near here

Cephalenia (kef-uh-len-*ee*-uh)

(modern Kefalonia) largest island in the Ionian Sea, very
close to Ithaca

ceramic (sir-*am*-ik)

clay which has been fired in a kiln, very hard and smooth

Charybdis (kuh-*rib*-diss)

mythological whirlpool encountered by Jason and his
men on their way home, thought to be in the straits of
Messina (between Sicily and the toe of Italy's boot); the
phenomenon of sulphurous gases causing water to 'boil'
and fish to die was documented as recently as 2003 in
these waters

Cnidos (k'*nee*-dos)

famous town with a double harbour on a promontory in
Asia Minor (Turkey)

Colchis (*cole*-kiss)

Jason's destination: the golden fleece was kept there,
guarded by a dragon

colonnade (call-a-*nade*)

a covered walkway lined with columns

Colossus of Rhodes (kuh-*loss*-iss)

gigantic statue of the sun god Helios made by Chares of
Lindos in the third century BC; in Roman times it was
admired as one of the Seven Wonders of the world even
though an earthquake toppled it 66 years after it was first
dedicated

Corinth (*kor*-inth)

busy commercial Greek port situated on an isthmus between the Ionian and Aegean seas; Nero's canal had been abandoned by Flavia's time, but ships could still be transported across the isthmus which was about four miles wide

Cos (*koss*)

(modern Kos) Greek island near Halicarnassus, it was the site of an important sanctuary of Aesculapius

Cyclops (*sigh*-klops)

mythical giants with only one eye in the centre of their foreheads

Cythnos (*kith*-noss)

island in the Aegean; also known as Thermia because of its famous hot springs

Delos (*dee*-loss)

tiny island in the Aegean Sea, the mythical birthplace of Apollo and centre of slave trade during the Roman Republic

denarius (den-*are*-ee-us)

small silver coin worth four sesterces

diolkos (dee-*ol*-koss)

a paved way with ruts to guide the wheels of carts carrying unloaded ships across the isthmus of Corinth at its narrowest point

Dionysus (dye-oh-*nie*-suss)

Greek god of vineyards and wine; he comforted Ariadne on Naxos

domina (*dom*-in-ah)

Latin for 'mistress' or 'madame'; a polite form of address for a woman

Dorian (*door*-ee-un)

   connected with the Doric-speaking Greeks who inhabited
   parts of mainland Greece as well as Crete and the
   southern coast of Asia (modern Turkey)

ephedron (*eff*-ed-ron)

   a plant mentioned by Pliny the Elder still used today in
   the treatment of asthma

Ephesus (*eff*-ess-iss)

   perhaps the most important town in the Roman province
   of Asia and site of one of the Seven Wonders of the
   Ancient World, the Temple of Diana

euge! (*oh*-gay)

   Latin exclamation: 'hurray!'

Euphemus (yoo-*fee*-muss)

   one of the argonauts; he sent the dove between the
   Clashing Rocks

ex voto (ex *vo*-to)

   object sometimes offered to a god or goddess when a
   vow is made

Flaccus (*flak*-uss)

   Gaius Valerius Flaccus, a poet who began a version of the
   Argonautica in AD 80

Flavia (*flay*-vee-a)

   a name, meaning 'fair-haired'; Flavius is another form of
   this name

forestay (*for*-stay)

   thick rope or cable which goes from the prow of a ship to
   the top of a mast in order to hold it up

Fortuna (for-*tew*-nuh)

   the Roman goddess of good luck and success

forum (*for*-um)

ancient marketplace and civic centre in Roman towns

freedman (*freed*-man)

a slave who has been granted freedom, his ex-master becomes his patron

Germania (jur-*man*-ya)

Roman province which included what is now Germany

Hades (*hay*-deez)

the Underworld where the spirits of the dead were believed to go

Halicarnassus (hal-ee-car-*nass*-uss)

(modern Bodrum) ancient city in the region of Caria and site of one of the Seven Wonders of the Ancient World, the Mausoleum of Halicarnassus

halyard (*hal*-yard)

rope to lift up flags or other ropes and especially the yard-arm

harpy (*har*-pee)

mythological bird with woman's head; it screeches and steals food

Hebrew (*hee*-brew)

language spoken by some religious Jews in the first century AD

Hector (*heck*-tor)

noblest son of Priam and greatest hero of Troy, he was killed by Achilles

Helios (*hee*-lee-oss)

although Apollo was god of the sun, Helios was the Titan who drove the sun across the sky in a chariot; *helios* is Greek for 'sun'

Hera (*here*-uh)

Greek goddess of childbirth and wife of Zeus, her Roman equivalent is Juno

Hercules (*her*-kyoo-leez)

mythological hero who completed twelve tasks; he was one of Jason's argonauts until his squire Hylas disappeared and he stayed behind to search for him

Horace (*hore*-uss)

famous Latin poet who lived during the reign of Augustus

hospitium (hoss-*pit*-ee-um)

Latin for hotel or guesthouse; often very luxurious with baths and dining rooms

Hylas (*hi*-lass)

beautiful youth who accompanied Hercules on the *Argo*; he was abducted by water nymphs and had to be left behind

Ionian (eye-*oh*-nee-un)

the sea between Italy and mainland Greece

isthmus (*isth*-muss)

narrow piece of land connecting two larger pieces of land

Ithaca (*ith*-uh-ka)

small island on the west coast of Greece and home of the hero Odysseus; his voyage home from Troy took him ten long years

Jason (*jay*-sun)

Greek hero who set out in the *Argo* with many heroes to steal the golden fleece and thus win back his rightful kingdom

Jove (jove)

another name for Jupiter, king of the gods

Juno (*jew*-no)

> queen of the gods and wife of the god Jupiter, her Greek equivalent is Hera

Jupiter (*jew*-pit-er)

> king of the Roman gods and husband of Juno; his Greek equivalent is Zeus

Lechaeum (*lek*-eye-um)

> western port of Corinth; one end of the *diolkos* was here

lemures (lem-*oo*-rays)

> shades or ghosts of dead people

lifts (*lifts*)

> short ropes from the top of the masthead; they hold up the yard-arm

lustratio (lus-*tra*-tee-oh)

> a ritual for purification of houses, ships, etc which may involve the sacrifice of a bull

Malea (mal-*lay*-uh)

> (or Cape Malea) southeast tip of mainland Greece; dreaded by sailors because of weather and pirates

Medea (m'-*dee*-ah)

> sorceress who loved Jason and betrayed her own people to help him

Mopsus (*mop*-suss)

> soothsayer and priest who accompanied Jason on his quest for the fleece

Myconos (*mick*-oh-noss)

> (modern Mykonos) island in the Aegean Sea

Neapolis (nay-*ap*-oh-liss)

> modern Naples, a city near Vesuvius on a bay of the same name

Nero (*near*-oh)

wicked Emperor who ruled Rome from AD 54 to AD 68

Odysseus (uh-*diss*-yooss)

Greek hero who fought against Troy; his journey home took ten years

Odyssey (*odd*-iss-ee)

Homer's Greek epic poem about Odysseus' voyage home

Orpheus (*or*-fee-uss)

mythological lyre-player who charmed men, animals and rocks with his music, he was one of Jason's argonauts

Ostia (*oss*-tee-uh)

the port of ancient Rome and home town of Flavia and Jonathan ben Mordecai

Ovid (*aw*-vid)

famous Roman poet who lived about 70 years before this story

palla (pal-uh)

a woman's cloak, could also be wrapped round the waist or worn over the head

papyrus (puh-*pie*-russ)

the cheapest writing material, made of pounded Egyptian reeds

Paris (*pair*-uss)

handsome Trojan prince who stole Helen of Sparta and started the Trojan War

Patmos (*pat*-mos)

small island in the Aegean which was a place of exile in Roman times; St John wrote the Book of Revelation here about fifteen years after this story takes place

patrician (pa-*trish*-un)

a person from the highest Roman social class

Patroclus (*pat*-ro-kluss)

Greek hero and best friend of Achilles, he was killed by the Trojan Hector

Peleus (*pel*-lay-uss)

father of the great Greek hero Achilles, one of Jason's argonauts

Pelias (*pel*-ee-uss)

deposed his brother (Jason's father) and seized his kingdom; when his nephew Jason arrived to reclaim it, he sent him on an 'impossible' quest

pharus (*far*-uss)

(Greek *pharos*) lighthouse; the famous lighthouse of Alexandria was one of the Seven Wonders of the ancient world

Phineus (*fin*-ee-uss)

mythological blind prophet from Thrace who was tormented by harpies

plebs (plebz)

the common people, the lowest class of freeborn Romans

Pliny (*plin*-ee)

(the Elder) famous Roman author; died in the eruption of Vesuvius

poculum (*pock*-yoo-lum)

a cup; here a liquid breakfast of goat's milk, egg, spiced wine, milk and honey

Pollux (*pol*-lux)

one of the mythological twins (he was immortal and Castor mortal); he was a skilled boxer and horseman, and also one of Jason's argonauts

Poseidon (poh-*side*-un)

Greek god of the sea, the equivalent of the Roman god Neptune

prow

pointed projecting front part of a ship; Romans often painted eyes on the prow

Ravenna (ruh-*ven*-uh)

seaport in northeast Italy where part of the Roman fleet was based

Rhodes (roads)

a large and famous island in the Aegean Sea, Rhodes was the capital of the Roman province of Asia at the time of this story

Rhoda (*road*-ah)

sea nymph daughter of Poseidon who married Helios; her name means 'rosy' in Greek and the island of Rhodes was called after her

Rhodes Town (roads town)

capital city of the island of Rhodes both then and now

scroll (skrole)

a papyrus or parchment 'book', unrolled from side to side as it was read

Scylla (*skill*-uh)

mythological monster with six terrible female heads, always found close to the whirlpool Charybdis; encountered by the argonauts on their way home

sesterces (sess-*tur*-seez)

more than one sestercius, a brass coin; four sesterces equal a denarius

Sirens (*sigh*-wrens)

mythological monsters with bodies of birds and heads of women; they sang beautifully, luring sailors to their death on sharp rocks

Skiron (*skeer*-on)

wind from the north-west which prevailed in the Mediterranean in the summer (see the Wind Map at the front of this book)

stern

back of a ship; Roman ships often had a platform with an altar and bird's head

Stoic (*stow*-ick)

a Greek philosophy popular in ancient Rome; among other things, its followers believed that a man's destiny was predetermined

strigil (*strig*-ill)

a blunt-edged, curved tool for scraping off dead skin, oil and dirt at the baths

stylus (*stile*-us)

a metal, wood or ivory tool for writing on wax tablets

Surrentum (sir-*ren*-tum)

modern Sorrento, a pretty harbour town south of Vesuvius

Symi (*sim*-ee)

small island near Rhodes famous for its sponge-divers

Syros (*seer*-oss)

one of the islands in the Aegean Sea

tablinum (tab-*lee*-num)

the study of a Roman house, where scrolls and writing material were kept

Talos (*tal*-oss)

bronze giant who attacked Jason and his men when they passed Crete

Telephus (*tell*-uh-fuss)

mythological son of Hercules, he was suckled by a deer

and rarely spoke, hence the common Roman expression 'silent as Telephus'

Tiphys (*tiff*-uss)

skilled helmsman who was one of Jason's argonauts

Titus (*tie*-tuss)

Titus Flavius Vespasianus; 41-year-old Emperor of Rome in AD 80

toga (*toe*-ga)

a blanket-like outer garment, worn by freeborn men and boys

triclinium (trick-*lin*-ee-um)

ancient Roman dining room, usually with three couches to recline on

tunic (*tew*-nic)

a piece of clothing like a big T-shirt; children often wore a long-sleeved one

Tyrrhenian (tur-*ren*-ee-un)

sea to the west of Italy, named after the Etruscans

Varro (*vah*-ro)

Publius Terentius Varro Atacinus, a Latin poet who translated the *Argonautica* of Apollonius into Latin

Vesuvius (vuh-*soo*-vee-yus)

the volcano near Naples which erupted on 24 August AD 79

Virgil (*vur*-jill)

a famous Latin poet who died about 100 years before this story takes place

votive (*vo*-tiv)

an object offered to mark a vow, prayer or thanksgiving to some god

vow

a pledge to a god or goddess which usually took the form 'If you do something for me, I will do something for you'; often the latter was the setting up of an altar

wax tablet

a wax-covered rectangular leaf of wood used for making notes; often two or more are hinged together with twine to make a 'book'

yard-arm

(or 'yard') the spar or piece of wood from which the sail of a ship is hung, it is usually horizontal and attached to the vertical mast

Zephyrus (*zef*-feer-uss)

a warm wind from the west, beloved of sailors (see the Wind Map at the front of this book)

Zetes (*zee*-teez)

argonaut and son of the North Wind Boreas, he had winged feet and could fly

Zeus (*zyooss*)

king of the Greek gods; his Roman equivalent is Jupiter

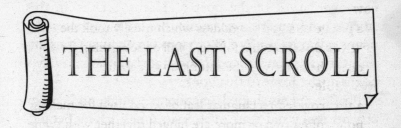

THE LAST SCROLL

Ancient Romans loved to travel just as much as we do today and the Colossus of Rhodes was on the list of monuments any rich Roman tourist had to see. The other six 'must-see' sights were the statue of Zeus at Olympia, the temple of Diana at Ephesus, the Hanging Gardens of Babylon, the Mausoleum of Halicarnassus, the Pyramids of Egypt and the Pharos (lighthouse) of Alexandria. At Roman dinner parties, returning travellers could impress their friends and rivals with tales of these Seven Wonders.

Today we look down on the ancient Romans because they enslaved other human beings, including children. But according to recent studies, there are over 27 million slaves – people who work for no pay against their will – in the world today. Many of these modern slaves are children forced to weave carpets in terrible conditions at the expense of their health and eyesight. (Find out more and learn how to fight modern slavery at the National Geographic website: http://magma.nationalgeographic.com/ngm/0309)

All the characters who appear in this story are fictional, except one. Gaius Valerius Flaccus was a young man when he began his own version of the *Argonautica* around AD 80, the year this story takes place.

However, most of the poetry Flaccus 'recites' in this story is not from his *Argonautica*, but is a paraphrase of a poem called *Ithaka* by the modern Greek poet Constantine Cavafy. You can read my translation of Cavafy's poem at the front of this book.

Phallic (penis-shaped) pendants, rings and other charms really did exist in Roman times. Many people, especially children, wore them for protection against evil spirits and bad luck. You can see them in many museums with Roman collections.